obscure
no more

AN INDUCTIVE BIBLE STUDY

obscure
no more

Life-Shaping Lessons from the Often Overlooked

LeAnne Blackmore

Standard® PUBLISHING

Cincinnati, Ohio

Published by Standard Publishing, Cincinnati, Ohio
www.standardpub.com

Printed in: United States of America
Substantive editor: Diane Stortz
Cover design: Brand Navigation
Interior design: Dina Sorn at Ahaa! Design

Photo credits: Maps and charts on pages 21–25 are taken from the *Standard Bible Atlas*. Copyright © 2006, 2008 by Standard Publishing. All rights reserved. Map of ancient Jerusalem on page 26 is taken from *Hurlbut's Bible Lessons*, by Rev. Jesse Lyman Hurlbut. Copyright © 1907 by The John C. Winston Co.

All Scripture quotations, unless otherwise indicated, are taken from the *HOLY BIBLE, NEW INTERNATIONAL VERSION®. NIV®.* Copyright © 1973, 1978, 1984 by Biblica, Inc.™ Used by permission of Zondervan. All rights reserved.
Scripture quotations marked (*NASB*) are taken from the *New American Standard Bible®*. Copyright © 1960, 1962, 1963, 1968, 1971, 1972, 1973, 1975, 1977, 1995 by The Lockman Foundation. Used by permission. (www.Lockman.org). All rights reserved.
Scripture quotations marked (*NLT*) are taken from the Holy Bible, *New Living Translation*. Copyright © 1996, 2004. Used by permission of Tyndale House Publishers, Inc., Wheaton, Illinois 60189. All rights reserved.
Scripture quotations marked (*The Message*) are taken from *THE MESSAGE*. Copyright © by Eugene H. Peterson 1993, 1994, 1995, 1996, 2000, 2001, 2002. Used by permission of NavPress Publishing Group.
Scripture quotations marked (*KJV*) are taken from the *King James Version.*

ISBN 978-0-7847-2572-6

Library of Congress Cataloging-in-Publication Data

Blackmore, LeAnne, 1966-
  Obscure no more : life-shaping lessons from the often overlooked / LeAnne Blackmore.
     p. cm.
  ISBN 978-0-7847-2572-6 (perfect bound)
  1. Christian life--Biblical teaching--Textbooks. 2. Bible--Textbooks. 3. Bible--Criticism, interpretation, etc. I. Title.
  BS680.C47B54 2010
  221.07--dc22
                        2010025606

15 14 13 12 11 10   1 2 3 4 5 6 7 8 9

CONTENTS

It was fascinating.

That Easter Sunday the choir sang an incredible song with lyrics describing the work of the Artist. At the front of the auditorium, one of our more artistic church members took brush to canvas and with sweeping motions applied black paint in a temporarily indistinguishable pattern. When the choir belted out the chorus, an image began to emerge. First, a crown of thorns. Next, a beard. Drops of blood flowing downward.

The face of Christ.

Then at the very last moment, with the choir holding a high note . . . the *expression* of my Savior changed! Slight brushstrokes left intricate markings, adding a soulful, compelling look on the face of my Jesus.

It was mesmerizing. I honestly cannot tell you what happened during the rest of the service, for my eyes were fixed on his face. My thoughts were on him . . . on his task . . . his emotions . . . his sacrifice . . . his love. I was caught off guard by the lessons God showed me with these strokes of paint. Broad brushstrokes and slight, intricate markings—both were necessary to create the artwork before me. Together they brought me closer to my God.

So it is with God's Word. God uses larger-than-life characters and stories to affect our hearts and draw us to himself. Abraham. Moses. David. Paul. If we add up all the chapters dedicated solely to these men, we can account for a large portion of the Bible. Much can be learned from them. These sweeping strokes give us, in many ways, the overview of God's plan and purpose. But not everyone in Scripture fills page after page from Genesis to Revelation. Some are less prominent . . . more obscure. They are the slight brushstrokes of humanity, preserved for you and me to add richness and depth to our understanding of God.

I wrote this study to share the stories of ten of the less prominent characters in

Scripture and to help us all learn life lessons that will deepen our relationship with our heavenly Father. God preserved the stories of these people for a purpose, to encourage us and give us hope (see Romans 15:4). Let this book be a tool for you to uncover these stories, make your own obscure observations (journal pages are included at the end of each chapter), or even lead a group to make discoveries together (Leader's Guide included at the end of the book). I pray that in doing this study you will be encouraged as these stories in Scripture come alive, that you'll see these formerly blurred accounts clearly, and that you'll be filled with hope when you realize how valuable to God's kingdom your own story can be. The Bible, these characters, and your own life will no longer seem so vague or difficult to understand. They will, in fact, be Obscure No More!

LeAnne Blackmore

getting started:
the Bible study process

My husband and I have had the privilege of traveling many places throughout the United States and around the world. On one of our first trips, we thought it would be fun to send our friend Tony a postcard. This quickly became a tradition, and on every subsequent trip we searched for the perfect card, one that best captured our experiences in that particular place. From shopping in San Francisco to caving in Turkey, we wanted Tony to enjoy a taste of each.

After twenty years Tony has filled a few photo albums with these picturesque postcards. But has he truly experienced the places they represent? He has more understanding of these places than before he received the cards, yet he doesn't have firsthand knowledge of the locales. He's never heard the sounds or smelled the scents or felt the breezes. He hasn't climbed the ruins, swum in the aqua seas, or savored the dishes specific to those lands.

My Postcard Prayer
Several years ago I realized my spiritual life was very much like Tony's books of postcards. I listened to preachers, sat in Sunday school classes, and read Christian books. Each time I heard a sermon, sat through a lesson, or read a chapter, it was as if I put a postcard in my own spiritual photo album. I caught glimpses of someone else's experience and saw snippets of another's relationship with the living God, but I didn't truly understand that firsthand knowledge. The real experience belonged to the preacher, the teacher, or the author. I merely received their postcards.

But that changed when I learned how to study the Bible.

A dear group of women at my church in Florida taught me how to study the Bible inductively, which is a simple process with profound impact. I soon found myself experiencing the Bible and the God of the Bible in a whole new way, as if my senses had awakened to taste and see and smell and hear and feel all of what God wanted for me! I understood God more deeply and more intimately. The words on the pages held meaning and life. For the first time I could *send* the postcard, so to speak. I wasn't dependent on someone else to go to the places in Scripture and capture what they found on a postcard to send to me. I could capture it on my own!

Instead of someone else telling you what God has to say, I want you to find out for yourself. That is my prayer for you . . . my postcard prayer.

God desires that you know him (Jeremiah 9:23, 24), that you seek him (Proverbs 8:17), and dig for yourself to mine the treasures in his Word (Psalm 119:162). When you do this, you will be the one sending the postcard! But more than that, you will truly know the one who created all the beauty captured on those cards.

What follows is an outline of the simple Bible study method that I learned. I pray you will invest time in reading and understanding the process, for that investment will yield great returns.

Enjoy your travels!

In each chapter of this Bible study, you will be guided through four different steps: *Read, Relate, Reflect,* and *Remember.* Each step is designed to reveal an aspect of God and his Word. This process of discovery and understanding is strengthened through the Holy Spirit's teaching and guidance (John 14:26; 16:13). So before you begin any study of the Word, pray and ask the Holy Spirit to lead you into truth. Once you have sought his leading, use the four steps to move you deeper into the Word: *Read, Relate, Reflect, Remember.*

Read

Sometimes we miss the obvious. But if we are going to study God's Word, it makes sense to read it. Too often we read books *about* the Bible instead of the Bible itself. So the first step is to read the passage you will study.

The purpose of the reading step is to discover things about the text. During this step you want to answer the question, What do I see? Play the role of a detective and get as much information as you can from the passage you are reading:

- Bombard the text with questions. Ask: Who? What? Where? When? Why? How?

- Determine the characters, the plot, and the setting.

- Discover the background, the historical stage.

- Look for repeated words or phrases. What does the author talk about the most?

- Are there any lists, contrasts, or comparisons?

- Note the timing or the sequence of events.

- Always remember to keep things in context.

Two great resources for the nitty-gritty details of inductive Bible study are *How to Study Your Bible* by Kay Arthur and *Living by the Book* by Howard G. Hendricks and William D. Hendricks. In *Living by the Book,* the authors give "Ten Strategies to First-Rate Reading." You might find their list helpful as you open your Bible to read:

- Read Thoughtfully

- Read Repeatedly

- Read Patiently

- Read Selectively

- Read Prayerfully

- Read Imaginatively

- Read Meditatively

- Read Purposefully

- Read Acquisitively

- Read Telescopically[1]

Let's look at the list item by item and, based on my reading of the Hendrickses' book and my own experience, I'll explain my understanding of each one.

Read Thoughtfully

In other words, get your mind into it. Oftentimes, I sit down to read and complete an entire page, only to realize my mind never engaged with the material! Schedules, grocery lists, deadlines . . . all seem to want my attention at that moment. Reading thoughtfully, however, requires that we shift our focus and concentrate on the task at hand.

Read Repeatedly

Scripture always amazes me! No matter how familiar I am with a passage, something new surfaces when I read it over again. Reading and rereading the Word is worthwhile and opens our eyes to fresh insights.

Read Patiently

Most people lack patience, especially given our immediate-results society. But patience in Bible study is a true asset. Bible study takes time. Learning how to learn takes time. We cannot expect to gain deep insights in a matter of minutes. So while you read, remember: it takes time to study, and it takes time to develop the craft of learning.

Read Selectively

Selective reading implies discernment. Our goal is to discern God's truth, so naturally we need to read with that in mind. Reading selectively, then, requires us to inundate the text with questions. Like any good detective, you need information. So when you are reading, ask yourself, Who? What? Where? When? Why? How?

Read Prayerfully

Howard Hendricks says, "We tend to think of Bible study and prayer as separate disciplines, but the fact is, they are integrally related."[2] I agree. Prayer is essential and the means to successful Bible study. Pray throughout the entire process. Bible study is about hearing from God, so it makes sense to carry on a dialogue with him. Talk with him when you are struggling to understand a passage. Be still and listen for him as he guides you into truth. And praise him when he shows you meaningful insights.

Read Imaginatively

"Variety is the spice of life." Adding variety to our Bible reading can spice up our study time as well. Imaginative reading allows us to be creative in our approach to Scripture. Vary the translations you read from. Read the passage out loud. Act it out. Write a script. Draw a picture representing the passage. Turn the verses into song lyrics. Get out of the monotony that sometimes pervades Bible reading.

Read Meditatively

Earlier I mentioned that we need to be thoughtful in our reading, engaging our minds as we read. Reading meditatively takes this one step further, requiring us to continue to think through what we've read. Mull it over. Let it simmer in the corners of your consciousness. This is a lost art, to be sure, but one that can open a new frontier in your studies.

Read Purposefully

God preserved every book, chapter, and verse in the Bible for a reason. Reading purposefully allows us to look for it. Why did the author write this particular book? What was his goal? Find answers to these questions by taking a closer look at the author's grammar and the book's literary structure. Observing these carefully leads to a more thorough understanding of the author's purpose.

Read Acquisitively

One goal of Bible study is life change. Getting into the Word is good . . . but getting the Word into us is best. For that to happen we need to read acquisitively—to take possession of the Word. Do whatever it takes to help you remember what you've read. Act it out. Rewrite it. Make charts. Develop character sketches or personality profiles. Become personally engaged and make the Bible your own.

Read Telescopically

"Telescopic reading means viewing the parts in light of the whole."[3] In other words, keep things in context. Remember, the books of the Bible together tell the story of God. The Bible is not a random collection of thoughts and stories haphazardly thrown together; it is a whole. When reading telescopically, keep in mind this question: What is the big picture?

Relate

In this second step of the process, we ask the question, What does it mean? We can relate the text first to the author and then to the whole counsel of Scripture.

Relate to the Author

Maybe you've heard, "You never truly know someone until you've walked a mile in his shoes." Relating to the author requires us to walk in his shoes. We want to re-create what he experienced. Can you feel what he felt? hear what he heard? see what he saw? get into the culture and the setting? In trying to understand the author's intent and perspective, we can better answer the question, What does it mean?

The following paragraphs outline some ways to get into the author's shoes and discover the meaning of the text.

Discover the occasion. Why was the author writing this? What prompted him? Oftentimes, the text itself has many clues that tell us why the author wrote the book.

Define the type of literature. Is it poetic? historical? biographical? a prophetic telling of future events or a collection of pithy proverbs? Understanding what kind of literature we are reading will make a big impact on how we interpret it. The content of a poetic song will be far different than that of a letter filled with principles of the faith. Each needs to be approached in the context of its literary style in order for accurate interpretation to take place.

Discern the meaning of the words. The original language of the Bible was not English. The Old Testament was written in Hebrew, the New Testament in Greek. Going back to the original language gives great insight into words and meanings that English doesn't fully express. You don't have to be a Hebrew or Greek scholar to do this. Greek is just that—Greek—to me, but many resources put the Hebrew and Greek definitions right at our fingertips! At points in the lessons, I'll show you some tools that will make these word studies possible.

Relate to the Whole Counsel of Scripture

The Bible is comprised of sixty-six books, the sum of which is a single unit. The theme is God's love story toward man and his redemptive plan for humankind. The Bible is God's revelation of truth, and although it was authored by men, their words were God-breathed (2 Timothy 3:16). Peter described this beautifully when he said, "Men spoke from God as they were carried along by the Holy Spirit" (2 Peter 1:21). Because the Bible is God's revelation and God's words, it is *inerrant*, free from error. Jesus himself bears witness to this in Matthew 5:17, 18. And throughout the Gospels Jesus constantly refers to Scripture, never questioning its accuracy, authority, or reliability. The Bible is completely trustworthy and without error in its original form. We can trust it as Jesus did.

Context is key. If I gave you a book with fractions in it, would you automatically assume it was a math book? That would be ridiculous, wouldn't it? Especially when you realized those fractions were measurements for ingredients in various recipes. You'd be holding a cookbook, not a math book. This is *context*, the environment in which we find something. Understanding the surroundings of the fractions would help determine the nature of the book. So it is with Scripture. We must understand the environment or surroundings of a passage in order to accurately interpret it. Taking things out of context makes for trouble. How many times have you seen this in the media? Someone gives an interview, and a short quote from that interview is spread all over, oftentimes completely misrepresenting the person who gave the interview because the context of the quote is not shared. The same holds true for Scripture. Many misunderstandings, misinterpretations, and even false religions have come about because the Word was taken out of context.

Familiarize yourself with the environment of the text. Consider the passage in light of the surrounding verses and chapters, the book in which the passage is found, and the entire counsel of the Word of God. Remember, context is key!

Cross-references are vital. The Bible never contradicts itself. Because of this, one of the best ways to illuminate a passage is to use Scripture to interpret Scripture. This is where cross-referencing comes into play. A *cross-reference* is a reference to another Scripture that supports, clarifies, or enhances the Scripture we are studying. Most subjects are not completely discussed in just one passage. Several verses, chapters, and books within the Bible might give insights into a topic. In order to get the complete picture, we need to study each reference where a subject is taught. Bits of truth can then be woven together to make the tapestry of that subject evident.

Commentaries can help. Having sought the Holy Spirit's leading and diligently applied ourselves to the task of studying, we will have a good grasp of the context and interpretation of a passage. Once we have read and related to the author and the whole counsel of Scripture, *then* we can consult *commentaries*, books, study notes, or articles that attempt to explain a text. Be aware that commentaries might reflect differing opinions, and don't be thrown off by this. It's nearly impossible for all of us to agree on every issue. That does not mean the Word itself is flawed; rather, our understanding of it is the thing that is faulty. We each approach Scripture with a variety of biases and opinions that can blur our objectivity.

Reading several different interpretations actually is a good way to determine if our objectivity is blurry. If anyone, commentators included, is completely off track, it will become apparent during this step. Kay Arthur says, "Be very wary if in your study you find something that no one else has ever seen before. God probably would not blind godly men to truth for almost 2,000 years and suddenly reveal it to you."[4] Commentaries are helpful, but always make certain the Word of God is your ultimate measuring stick!

I realize this may seem a little overwhelming. It's kind of like eating an elephant—you do it one bite at a time. We cannot endeavor to understand the Bible (or large chunks of it) in one attempt! Start with smaller portions and keep at it. A lot can be accomplished with methodical, manageable steps.

And before we move on from this *Relate* phase, let me offer one more bit of advice. Apply the KISS principle (Keep It Simple, Stupid!). By keeping things simple in my own Bible study and not seeking to mine the mother lode in my first exploration of a text, I have found many nuggets of truth worth treasuring. This KISS principle might be one you'll want to adopt as well; rather than unearthing frustration that prompts you to quit, you might find yourself inspired and motivated to carry on.

Reflect

"Anyone who listens to the word but does not do what it says is like a man who looks at his face in a mirror and, after looking at himself, goes away and immediately forgets what he looks like. But the man who looks intently into the perfect law that gives freedom, and continues to do this, not forgetting what he has heard, but doing it—he will be blessed in what he does" (James 1:23-25).

The third step of the Bible study process asks the question: How does this apply to my life? In our study we want to both *reflect on* the Word and *reflect* the Word *to* others.

Reflect on the Word

Considering the fact that we have read the text, bombarded it with questions, and re-created the author's experience to understand and interpret his writings, there should be much to think about! Reflecting on the Word now is the natural progression of Bible study.

Reflecting requires time—time to carefully consider what has been studied. The pondering has purpose, though, and that is life change. It is not enough to study and gain knowledge. We must put into action what we have learned.

Reflect the Word

I heard Louie Giglio, founder of Passion Conferences, give a powerful illustration on the idea of reflection. Louie explained that the bright moon we see in the night sky is really just a dark ball of dirt and dust; it does not produce or emit its own light. The sun reflecting off the moon gives the moon its light. The moon looks the brightest when it is directly aligned with the sun.

The same can be said of us. God formed man from the dust of the earth. We are sinners in need of a Savior (Romans 3:23; 7:18). But when we align ourselves in the path of the Son, his light reflects off us and makes us shine like stars in the universe (Philippians 2:15; 2 Corinthians 3:18).

Reflecting the Word means our lives reveal the transformation of Christ in us. It means allowing Jesus to have his way with us—changing our hearts, our beliefs, our attitudes, thoughts, and behaviors. It means wholehearted devotion and complete obedience. Picking and choosing the parts of the Bible that we find palatable is a cafeteria kind of Christianity. God is not calling us to do only the things that are pleasing to us but to embrace the things that are pleasing to him (2 Corinthians 5:9). He is looking for 100 percent surrender of our will to his. And James reminds us that those who are doers will find blessing in what they do.

So go on . . . shine! Reflect the Word. Emit Jesus Christ to the world around you! People everywhere need him too.

Remember

The last step in the Bible study process is to remember. In other words, we want to hide God's Word in our heart (Psalm 119:11).

One of my favorite chapters in the Bible is Psalm 119. The author, David, goes into great detail about the Word, its value, and our attitude toward it. Here is a sampling of what he says:

. . . .

How can a young man keep his way pure? By living according to your word. (v. 9)

Your statutes are my delight; they are my counselors. (v. 24)

I remember your ancient laws, O LORD, and I find comfort in them. (v. 52)

> Your commands make me wiser than my enemies, for they are ever with me. (v. 98)

> Great peace have they who love your law, and nothing can make them stumble. (v. 165)

. . . .

Purity. Counsel. Comfort. Wisdom. Peace. These are just a sampling of the benefits of the Word of God in our lives! There is so much more God intends for us to receive when we study and remember his Word. So how do we remember it? We've got to memorize it.

I know that for adults the admonition to memorize is a bit daunting. We feel our brain doesn't work that way anymore. God commands that we do this, however, so I'm asking that each week you find at least one verse from our study that has spoken to you, write that verse out, and work on getting it into your heart. Carry it around on an index card. Post it on a note on your bathroom mirror. Make it your screen saver and let the words scroll across your computer for the week. Find creative ways to keep God's Word before you, and you'll be surprised how the Word will begin to get into your mind and your heart. Then when you need encouragement, counsel, wisdom, peace, or hope, the Holy Spirit will bring a verse to mind and use it to minister to you and those around you.

·········●❍●·········

I don't know about you, but I'm excited to begin our study! God has a plan and a purpose for us through his Word and in particular through the stories of these obscure characters of old. Isaiah 55:11 says, "So is my word that goes out from my mouth: It will not return to me empty, but will accomplish what I desire and achieve the purpose for which I sent it." God will use his Word to accomplish his purpose in your life as we go through this study together. And God loves you with an everlasting love (Jeremiah 31:3)—so I know his purpose for you is a great one!

The following pages provide some maps and information that might be useful to you as you seek to understand the stories of these people who lived so long ago.

Timeline of Old Testament Events

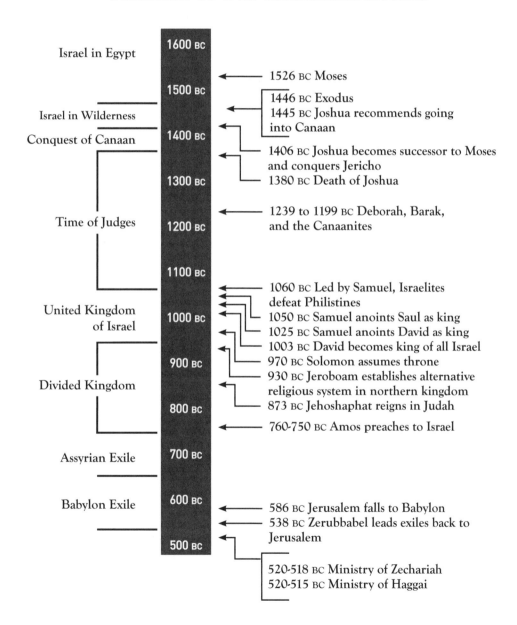

Israel in Egypt

1600 BC

← 1526 BC Moses

1500 BC

1446 BC Exodus
1445 BC Joshua recommends going
into Canaan

Israel in Wilderness

Conquest of Canaan

1400 BC

1406 BC Joshua becomes successor to Moses
and conquers Jericho
1380 BC Death of Joshua

1300 BC

1239 to 1199 BC Deborah, Barak,
and the Canaanites

Time of Judges

1200 BC

1100 BC

1060 BC Led by Samuel, Israelites
defeat Philistines
1050 BC Samuel anoints Saul as king

United Kingdom
of Israel

1000 BC

1025 BC Samuel anoints David as king
1003 BC David becomes king of all Israel
970 BC Solomon assumes throne

900 BC

930 BC Jeroboam establishes alternative
religious system in northern kingdom
873 BC Jehoshaphat reigns in Judah

Divided Kingdom

800 BC

760-750 BC Amos preaches to Israel

Assyrian Exile

700 BC

Babylon Exile

600 BC

586 BC Jerusalem falls to Babylon
538 BC Zerubbabel leads exiles back to
Jerusalem

500 BC

520-518 BC Ministry of Zechariah
520-515 BC Ministry of Haggai

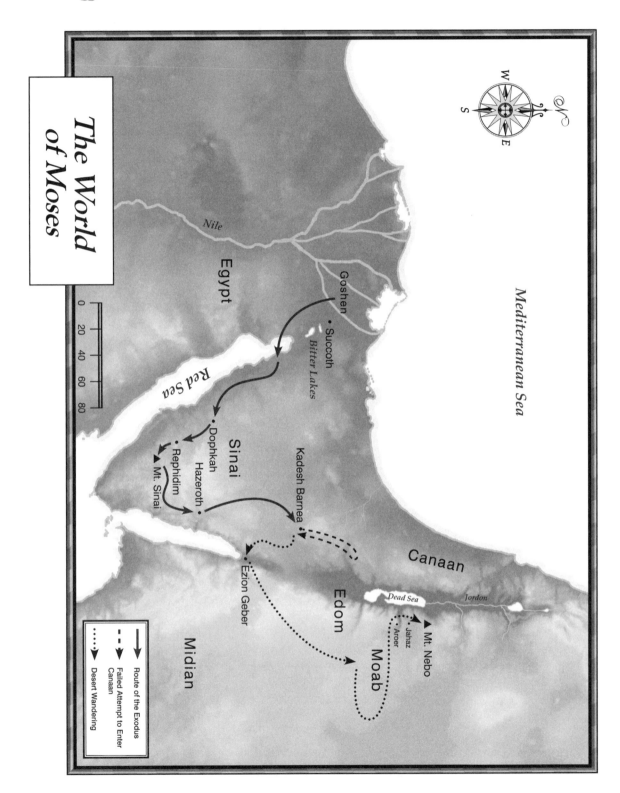

The World
of Moses

Judges of Israel

Judge	Major Oppressor	Years as Judge
Othniel (Judges 3:8-11)	Mesopotamia (Cushan-Rishathaim)	1373-1334 B.C.
Ehud (Judges 3:12-30)	Moabites (Eglon)	1319-1239 B.C.
Shamgar (Judges 3:31)	Philistines	1300 B.C.
Deborah (Judges 4, 5)	Canaanites (Jabin)	1239-1199 B.C.
Gideon (Judges 6–8)	Midianites	1192-1152 B.C.
Abimelech (Judges 9)	Period of Civil War	1152-1150 B.C.
Tola (Judges 10:1, 2)	Ammonites	1149-1126 B.C.
Jair (Judges 10:3-5)	Ammonites	1126-1104 B.C.
Jephthah (Judges 10:6–12:7)	Ammonites	1086-1080 B.C.
Ibzan (Judges 12:8-10)	Philistines	1080-1075 B.C.
Elon (Judges 12:11, 12)	Philistines	1075-1065 B.C.
Abdon (Judges 12:13-15)	Philistines	1065-1058 B.C.
Samson (Judges 13–16)	Philistines	1075-1055 B.C.
Eli (1 samuel 1–4)	Philistines	1107-1067 B.C.
Samuel (1 Samuel 7–9)	Philistines	1067-1043 B.C.

From Slavery to Slavery
(Chronology of Exodus to Exile)

Era	Leaders	Dates
Exodus and Wandering	Moses	1447-1407 B.C.
Conquest and Settlement	Joshua	1407-1380 B.C.
Judges	(see Chart 5)	1380-1050 B.C.
United Kingdom		1050-931 B.C.
	Saul	1050-1010 B.C.
	David	1010-970 B.C.
	Solomon	970-931 B.C.
Divided Kingdom		931-722 B.C.
	19 Kings of Israel 12 Kings of Judah 1 Queen of Judah	
Judah Alone	7 kings	722-586 B.C.
Captivity		604-538 B.C.

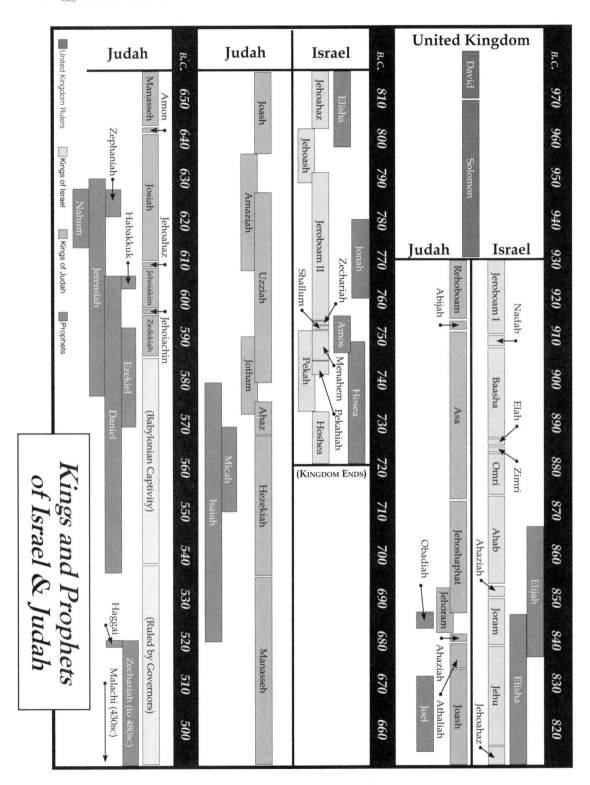

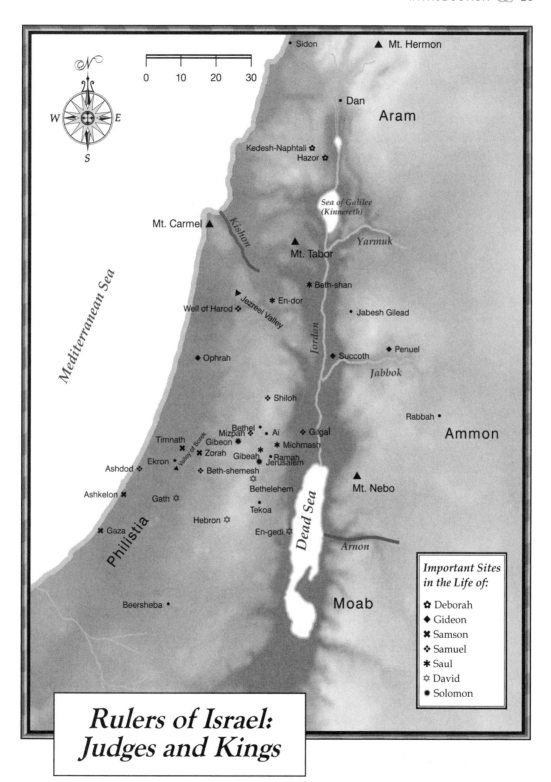

N
W   E
S

0   10   20   30

- Sidon
▲ Mt. Hermon
- Dan
Aram

Kedesh-Naphtali ✿
Hazor ✿

Sea of Galilee (Kinnereth)

Mt. Carmel ▲
Kishon
▲ Mt. Tabor
Yarmuk

✱ Beth-shan
▶
Jezreel Valley ✱ En-dor
Well of Harod ✿
- Jabesh Gilead

Jordan

◆ Ophrah
✱ Succoth
◆ Penuel

Jabbok

✤ Shiloh

Rabbah •

Mediterranean Sea

Bethel
• Ai
✤ Gilgal
Ammon

Mizpah ✿
Timnath
Valley of Sorek
Gibeon ✱
✱ Michmash
Ekron ✱ Zorah
Gibeah
• Ramah
Ashdod ✿
▲
Beth-shemesh
Jerusalem
✿
Ashkelon ✖
Bethelehem
Mt. Nebo ▲
Gath ✿
Tekoa
Gaza ✖
Hebron ✿
En-gedi ✿
Arnon

Phillstia

Dead Sea

Beersheba •

Moab

Important Sites in the Life of:

✿ Deborah
◆ Gideon
✖ Samson
✤ Samuel
✱ Saul
✿ David
✱ Solomon

Rulers of Israel: Judges and Kings

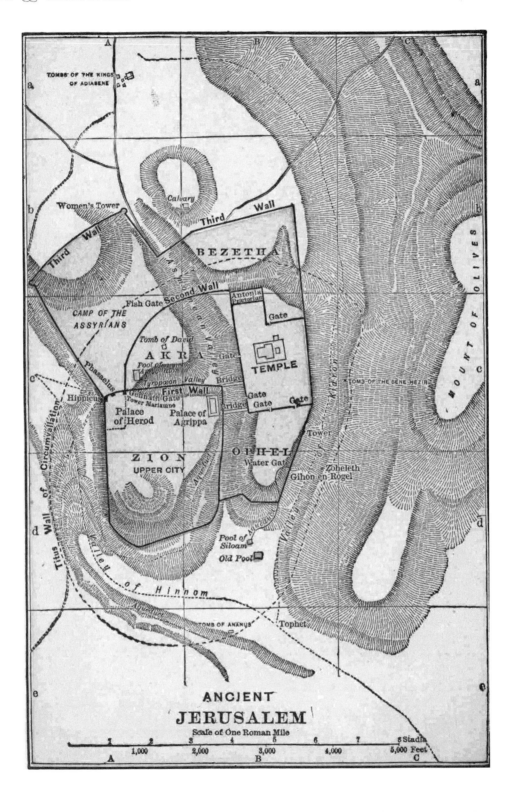

ANCIENT

JERUSALEM

Scale of One Roman Mile

CHAPTER ONE

Your halo only has to slip a few inches to become a noose.
—Anonymous

korah & company:
a rebellious brood

RESTRAINING YOUR PRIDE • NUMBERS 16:1-40

Bad Fads

From Beanie Babies to bell–bottoms, we've all been part of short-lived trends and sucked into the contagion that accompanies them. Did you do Tae Bo with Billy Blanks? Carry a back-pocket comb to make sure your feathered hair rivaled Farrah's or Fonzie's? Have you ever attempted to plaster on a pair of skinny jeans? Did you pay good money for brand-new sweatshirts and tank tops, only to cut them up with scissors? (That's what it took to have the coveted *Flashdance* look, remember?) Did you have a Cabbage Patch doll? Rubik's Cube? Lava lamp or mood ring?

If you could resurrect any of the following vogue trends, which would you prefer?

- The grunge look. Remember this? A wardrobe supplied solely from thrift stores and dumpsters. The more worn-out and baggy, the better. I know of some who spent more money at the local vending machine than they did for their "Sunday best"!

- String art. Beautiful artwork created by . . . you! These kits enabled you to make your own displayable art by taking string and winding it around nails set into a black-velvet background. Plain pieces of plywood worked too . . . at least in the circles my family hung around. Oh so pretty.

- Pet rocks. Surely you and your family had one of these, or several, because they were such low-maintenance pets! Your pet rock came with a care and training manual and a cardboard box home, complete with airholes and a soft straw bed.

- Baby on Board signs. Suctioned to the back window of your car, these alerted other drivers to your precious cargo to deter tailgating. You may remember other quickly marketed signs spoofing the original, including Baby I'm Bored and Mother-in-Law in Trunk.

And then there was streaking. Running naked in front of large crowds for the purpose of . . . frankly, I'm not sure why! I do remember watching the closing ceremonies of the 1976 Olympics and being exposed—literally—to Michael Leduc. He boldly ran (naked) where no man had run before.[5] I was ten years old and thought it was the funniest thing I had ever seen. Always the one to put a smile on my family's faces, I decided I would try streaking myself. I just had to wait for the right time.

Several days later, after returning home from an outing, I slipped into my bedroom and promptly slipped *out* of my clothing—all of it! Then I ran through the house yelling, "Streaker! Streaker!" My brother, lying on the couch, caught the first sight of me and burst into a raucous belly laugh. My mom, not quite sure what all the pandemonium was about, bounded into the kitchen and stopped me on my second lap. Grabbing hold of my little naked body, she planted a spanking on my bare behind.

"What do you think you are doing?" she exclaimed.

I ran back into my room and looked in the mirror at the red handprint on my backside. What *was* I thinking?

The same question can be posed to us. What are we thinking when we buy into these fads, crazes, and trends—when we emulate less-than-lucid behavior? I'm sure we could cite many reasons, whether emotional, psychological, or spiritual. And whether we agree on those reasons, I believe we all have to admit there is something infectious about fads. Something contagious.

Some contagions are funny and harmless, but others can be more severe. Remember reading in your history books about the McCarthy era? An attitude of fear infected our society and resulted in a Communist witch hunt within America's borders. Emotions and opinions can be infectious too. Both negative and positive, our feelings and judgments surrounding superstars and political candidates change with the wind. Often it is our conversations with others and the inundation of media coverage that affect and infect our thinking. Just track the polls; the numbers differ daily.

Then there are tangible contagions—bacteria and viruses. As I'm writing this, the world is experiencing a strain of flu called H1N1 or swine flu, which is extremely contagious and sometimes deadly. Schools, commercials, and press conferences have advised and reiterated precautionary measures.

Yes, fads, emotions, and illnesses can all be contagious. Yet something else can rear its ugly head and infect us all—sin. Sinful attitudes and actions can infiltrate the lives of even the most highly respected individuals. In this week's study we'll look at a man whose infectious opinions had an ill effect not only on himself but also on those in the upper echelon of Israel's camp. His influence started a craze . . . a trend . . . a fad—a sin sickness called rebellion.

Because we're talking about things that are contagious, let's approach this lesson from a medical perspective. We've all experienced trips to the doctor's office, so I've labeled our study processes with medical terminology. We will *Read* to get the patient history and *Relate* to consider the symptoms and diagnose the disease we're dealing with. We will treat the symptoms with specific prescriptions as we *Reflect*, and our follow-up appointment will be our time to *Remember*.

DAY ONE: READ
Patient History

1. Read Numbers 16:1-40.

2. When you go to the doctor's office, you typically have to answer some basic questions first thing. Patient name? Occupation? Medical history? Chief complaint? The doctor then uses this information to assess your situation. We're going to do the same thing here regarding Korah and his associates—"Korah & Company." Answer the following questions based on your reading:

Patient name: What is the main character's name? Who are his cohorts?

Occupation: Describe the work and responsibilities of Korah & Company.

How are the 250 men described?

Chief complaint: What complaint did Korah & Company make, and against whom?

What physical response did Moses give?

Warning Signs

I know when I'm getting a cold; I get this little tickle in the back of my throat. It's not unbearable, but it *is* noticeable and irritating. I hate it because I know what's in store. At that point, zinc and nasal saline become my new best friends. Trying to ward off anything that is attempting to bring me down is my number-one goal. Sometimes it works. Sometimes it doesn't.

Usually discernment comes quickly. When my head gets stuffy and the coughing begins, I know something is mounting an attack against my normally healthy body. Then the runny nose materializes, and before you know it my eyes are watery and my energy dissipates—all signs that something is awry.

Something was awry in Israel's camp. An adversarial attitude was escalating and a war was rising—from within. Who did Moses and Aaron think they were, anyway? God was clearly with *all* the people. Each day he manifested his presence in the pillar of cloud, and at night he displayed his glory through fire. Over and over the Israelites were told that God was in their midst, and they experienced firsthand his miracles and his judgments. So why did Moses feel the need to set himself up over all the people?

Who was he, anyway? Korah, Dathan, and Abiram discussed these things often and at length.

"He's my cousin, for goodness' sake!" Korah yelled. "What sets him apart any more than the rest of us?"

Dathan nodded. "He certainly hasn't done what he said he was going to do. Weren't we supposed to be in a land 'flowing with milk and honey' by now?"

"No milk. No honey. No way he should be in charge!" Abiram chimed in. "For all we know, his great plan is to leave us here so we can all die in this blasted wilderness!"

Over time the three became increasingly insolent. Interjecting rude and derogatory comments about their leaders at every turn, they began affecting those around them with their attitudes. Prominent men. Respected men. Men of the assembly. Men who would do well leading Israel, a nation of weary, worn-out wanderers. This nation needed new leadership *now*, they decided.

The group consisting of Korah, Dathan, Abiram, and 250 other prominent leaders agreed: the current leadership had to be confronted. Standing before Moses and Aaron, they let loose with their ammunition: "You have gone too far! The whole community is holy, every one of them, and the Lord is with them. Why then do you set yourselves above the Lord's assembly?" (Numbers 16:3).

Was Moses completely blindsided by this opposition? I doubt it. By this time, Moses had been leading the people of Israel for several years and had experienced his people at their worst. They were a contentious lot, a chronically complaining crew. In the book of Numbers alone, we see a pattern of griping and complaining . . . and results that should have put a damper on their communal irritability!

- Numbers 11:1 tells us that shortly after the Israelites began their journey to the promised land, the people complained about their hardships. The result—God sent fire as punishment.

In Numbers 11:4 we see that the people whined for quail, tired of God's abundant provision of manna. Bring on the meat! God gave them what they wanted—tons of it, in fact (v. 31). And while they gorged greedily on the quail, God sent a plague that sent many to their graves (v. 33).

Numbers 14:1-4, 20-24 tells us that the Israelites were tired of being stuck in the wilderness and wanted desperately to go to their promised land. But when they heard about giants living there, the Israelites whined and begged not to go in—they wanted to return to Egypt! God's response? He promised that all who complained would not be allowed to enter the promised land . . . *ever*! Rather, their descendants would be the ones to experience it.

The Israelites' pattern of whining, complaining, and thinking they knew best hadn't brought good results. But this new complaint was different, right? These were the prominent, renowned leaders bringing their case before Moses and Aaron. They had validated one another's arguments and nurtured the dissension. Certainly they could do a better job than the current leadership. Or should they have viewed their discontent and unrest as a warning sign—a tickle in the back of their collective throat? A tickle that would lead to unhealthy, prideful attitudes and full-on rebellion against the one who knew best.

OBSCURE
Bible Facts

The Hebrew word for "leaders" (*nasiy*, 5387) comes from the root word meaning "to exalt oneself" (*nasa*, 5375). It's interesting then to note that the leaders in this story are the ones bringing this charge of exalting oneself against Moses and Aaron in verse 3.

Ignoring all the warning signs, Korah & Company moved forward with their plan.

DAY TWO: READ
Patient History—Part 2

1. Read Numbers 16:1-40 again. At some point during the day, retell the story to someone else (a family member, neighbor, or friend). Who will that be? Write the name of that person here.

2. Because of Korah's complaint against Moses and Aaron, a showdown ensued. Where did it take place?

   How did God show up?

   What was God's initial response to the group?

   Who intervened?

What was the litmus test to prove Moses was indeed God's chosen leader?

3. Describe what happened to Korah, Dathan, and Abiram.

4. How did the people respond?

5. What happened to the 250 men?

6. What did God want done to the censers? Why?

Doctor's Orders

Immediately, Moses sensed the sickness. He saw the haughtiness and heard the pride. He fell facedown in an act of humility before the God whom these men were rebuffing.

Moses understood that by rejecting him as their leader they were actually rejecting God himself (Numbers 16:11). And as in the past, Moses knew God would be the one to diagnose and treat the disease.

Take 250 Censers and Call Me in the Morning

Until that happened, Moses gave a directive: "You, Korah, and all your followers are to do this: Take censers and tomorrow put fire and incense in them before the LORD. The man the LORD chooses will be the one who is holy. You Levites have gone too far!" (Numbers 16:6, 7).

Moses then went on to call out Korah and the other Levites for snubbing the special assignment God had already given them. "Now listen, you Levites! Isn't it enough for you that the God of Israel has separated you from the rest of the Israelite community and brought you near himself to do the work at the LORD's tabernacle and to stand before the community and minister to them? He has brought you and all your fellow Levites near himself, but now you are trying to get the priesthood too" (Numbers 16:8-10).

You see, in God's plan, the Levites had been separated out from the other tribes to perform special duties. The designated tasks (Numbers 3:6-9) included assisting Aaron and his sons—the priests—with servicing the tabernacle, the tent where God dwelled among the Israelites (Exodus 25:8; 40:34-37). These duties required the utmost respect toward God, his priests, and his dwelling place the tabernacle; the position required great humility and great service. Evidently, though, this group of men thought the calling of God on their lives was beneath them. They aspired to have more. They aspired to have Aaron's position.

After finishing his lecture to Korah and the Levites, Moses turned his attention toward Dathan and Abiram. However, these two yellow-bellied cowards wouldn't show up before Moses. After sharing his outrage with God, Moses reiterated the command to Korah & Company to show up with their censers in the morning.

Flatlined

Korah and his rebellious cohorts took their fire-filled censers in hand and stood in opposition to Moses and Aaron at the entrance to the tabernacle. Now God showed up, and he'd had enough! Ready to destroy all the people, he told Moses and Aaron to separate themselves from the people so he could get rid of them all at once!

Always the intercessors, Moses and Aaron fell on their faces and pleaded for God to take care of the one who infected the camp with sin. But God knows the hearts and minds of all, and he called not only for Korah but for Dathan and Abiram as well.

Upon commanding everyone to back away from the tents of these men, Moses delivered the litmus test. If God had not truly chosen Moses to be the leader of Israel, then Korah, Dathan, and Abiram would die a natural death. But if God had sent Moses to be their leader, then something completely new would happen to these guys . . . like, say, the ground opening up and swallowing them alive, along with all their belongings. And guess what? A totally new thing happened that day. God caused the earth to open up and swallow the men and their belongings into the grave.

Case closed. Moses was God's man. Any questions?

Obviously, panic broke out; all the people feared they were next! But it wasn't everyone who had shown contempt for God. It was Korah, Dathan, Abiram . . . and the 250 other leaders. With the first three taken care of, God now dealt with the others—with fire. Ironic, huh? They were attempting to offer fire to the Lord—and he used fire to destroy them. God wasn't playing around. When he said the priests were the only ones to offer fire, he meant it.

The men were flatlined.

The infectious rebellion was held in check.

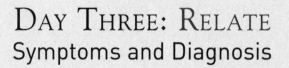

DAY THREE: RELATE
Symptoms and Diagnosis

Whenever you have an illness or a disease, there are usually symptoms that arise. The same is true of sin. Korah & Company displayed a variety of symptoms indicative of their sin sickness.

1. Read through Numbers 16:1-40 again, looking for possible symptoms of Korah's disease, such as anger and jealousy (v. 3).

2. Read what these verses say about the following symptoms and write what you learn in the space provided:

Symptom: irritability, discontent, ungratefulness. Numbers 16:8-10, 13, 14; 17:10.

Symptom: being argumentative. Numbers 16:3; Isaiah 45:9.

Symptom: hearing loss. Isaiah 30:9.

KORAH & COMPANY: A REBELLIOUS BROOD 39

Symptom: "big head" syndrome. Isaiah 14:12-14; 30:1; 1 Timothy 3:6.

Symptom: memory loss. Nehemiah 9:17.

3. Based on the symptoms in the two previous questions, what would you say is the diagnosis?

Read Jude 11 to confirm your analysis.

Pride's Prognosis

"Feeling their oats." "Too big for their britches." "All puffed up." Pick your descriptor. They all point to the same problem: an inflated ego, a big head, pride. And Korah & Company fit the bill. Not surprisingly, God's Word gives a specific prognosis where pride is involved: "Pride goes before destruction, a haughty spirit before a fall" (Proverbs 16:18).

We've seen this played out time and again. The Bible is strewn with characters who fell hard because of pride: Samson, Saul, and Nebuchadnezzar, just to name a few. Modern history tells tales about similar moral collapses: look at Napoleon, Hitler, or even Saddam Hussein.

Remember former presidential candidate John Edwards? For months he denied having an affair with one of his campaign employees, only to share later in an interview with ABC's Bob Woodruff that he had indeed been unfaithful to his spouse. Interestingly, Edwards blamed the affair on the praise and adoration he had received from his quick ascension into presidential politics. "I went from being a senator, a young senator, to being considered for vice president, running for president, being a vice-presidential candidate, and becoming a national public figure. All of which fed a self-focus, an egotism, a narcissim that leads you to believe that you can do whatever you want. You're invincible. And there will be no consequences."[6]

And if we believe we're immune to this, we need to reevaluate. The apostle Paul wanted to make sure we understood that pride can infect us all: "So, if you think you are standing firm, be careful that you don't fall!" (1 Corinthians 10:12). As a matter of fact, in his letter to the Corinthians, Paul uses many stories from the book of Numbers as "examples to keep us from setting our hearts on evil things as they did" (v. 6). He wanted us to learn from the Israelites' mistakes.

Speaking of learning from mistakes . . . one of my favorite TV shows is TLC's *What Not to Wear*. Fashion gurus Stacy London and Clinton Kelly swoop in on unsuspecting women (and sometimes men) who are surprisingly unaware of their egregious fashion faux pas. At the beginning of each episode, one pitiful prospect stands in a 360-degree mirror, wearing combinations of clothing she considers worthy of public view. Stacy and Clinton then offer a few choice words about the outfits. Once they have verbally obliterated their client's wardrobe, Stacy and Clinton review rules for clothing appropriate for her unique style and body shape. The goal: arm this individual with rules (and money!) for purchasing suitable, stylish clothing so she can set the fashion example and no longer be the poster child for what not to wear.

Korah's issue wasn't fashion, but he certainly left an example for what not to do. I don't know about you, but I'd rather learn from his mistakes than forge a rocky path of my own. And there's a huge lesson to be learned from Korah when it comes to dealing with pride. The number-one rule for what not to do: don't reject God's authority.

Moses and Aaron were the established leadership, and the establisher was God. "He sent Moses his servant, and Aaron, whom he had chosen" (Psalm 105:26). Moses had not chosen this task; God had chosen Moses to lead his people out of bondage in Egypt. The calling took place in God's presence, before a burning bush, on holy ground. Moses, a Hebrew raised in Pharoah's household, had run away from Egypt because of sin in his own life. When God called him, he was a shepherd with forty years' experience leading sheep in a wilderness—grand training for one who would spend another forty years leading God's flock through their own wilderness. "So now, go. I am sending you to Pharaoh to bring my people the Israelites out of Egypt. . . . I will be with you. And this will be the sign to you that it is I who have sent you: When you have brought the people out of Egypt, you will worship God on this mountain. . . . This is what you are to say to the Israelites: 'I AM has sent me to you'" (Exodus 3:10, 12, 14).

Moses wasn't the only one chosen by God to lead. Concerning Aaron, God said, "He will speak to the people for you, and it will be as if he were your mouth and as if you were God to him" (Exodus 4:16).

Throughout their leadership stint, God also made it clear that he was communicating directly to these men.

· ·

The LORD spoke to Moses in the Tent of Meeting in the Desert of Sinai on the first day of the second month of the second year after the Israelites came out of Egypt. (Numbers 1:1)

The LORD said to Moses and Aaron. . . . (Numbers 2:1; 4:1, 17)

This is the account of the family of Aaron and Moses at the time the LORD talked with Moses on Mount Sinai. (Numbers 3:1)

The LORD said to Moses. . . . (Numbers 3:40; 4:21; 5:1; 6:1, 22; 8:1, 5)

When Moses entered the Tent of Meeting to speak with the LORD, he heard the voice speaking to him from between the two cherubim above the atonement cover on the ark of the Testimony. And he spoke with him. (Numbers 7:89)

So Moses went out and told the people what the LORD had said. (Numbers 11:24)

. . . .

You can see by these verses (not an exhaustive list by any means!) that God was clearly communicating with his chosen leaders. At one point, Miriam (Moses' sister) and Aaron challenged Moses' leadership themselves, and God made it known that he had an intimate relationship with Moses: "When a prophet of the LORD is among you, I reveal myself to him in visions, I speak to him in dreams. But this is not true of my servant Moses; he is faithful in all my house. With him I speak face to face, clearly and not in riddles; he sees the form of the LORD. Why then were you not afraid to speak against my servant Moses?" (Numbers 12:6-8).

Should it have been clear, then, to Korah & Company that this man Moses and his brother Aaron were God's men? Absolutely! Then why did they reject God's authority?

I guess we should ask ourselves the same question. Why *do* we reject God's authority? God has spoken directly to us through his Word. Everything we need pertaining to life and godliness can be found in the pages of Scripture (2 Peter 1:3). Jesus defined Scripture as the truth (John 17:17). Paul tells us that "all Scripture is God-breathed" (2 Timothy 3:16). Yet we question Scripture's authority. We opt out of certain commands and principles, pick and choose what we find palatable, and then discard those things that rub us the wrong way.

The Barna Group recently published findings regarding Americans' attitudes toward the Bible. One startling statistic shows 43 percent of the random sampling polled agreed that the Bible, the Koran, and the Book of Mormon offer the same spiritual truths. The percentage is even higher, 56 percent, for those in the eighteen to twenty-five age range.[7]

In another survey regarding ways of experiencing God, 71 percent of those polled said they were more likely to develop their religious beliefs on their own than to accept an entire set of beliefs taught by a particular church.[8]

For years our culture has been exhibiting a spiritual cafeteria mentality, a have-it-your-way belief system. In 2002 actress Sarah Michelle Gellar, star of the TV show *Buffy the Vampire Slayer*, said, "I consider myself a spiritual person. I believe in an idea of God, although it's my own personal ideal. I find most religions interesting, and I've been to every kind of denomination: Catholic, Christian, Jewish, Buddhist. I've taken bits from everything and customized it."[9]

Unfounded, ungrounded confidence that we know better than God is a prideful, contentious attitude, and we know about pride and its prognosis now, don't we? "Pride goes before destruction, a haughty spirit before a fall" (Proverbs 16:18).

OBSCURE
Bible Facts

The pride of Korah and his colleagues brought them down to the grave. The Hebrew word for this place was *Sheol*. Though this place has a variety of meanings depending on its usage, in general it was considered to be a dwelling place for the dead.

········●◗◖●·········

DAY FOUR: REFLECT
The Prescription

1. In the list of symptoms of rebellion that follows, you will find with each symptom a scriptural comment about this symptom, a scriptural prescription you can use to treat the problem, and an opportunity for self-examination. Read the verses and highlight the action prescribed. Once you have figured out the exact prescription for the symptom, do a self-examination. How are you faring in this area? Is there an action step you can take to help remedy the problem? If so, write it down.

Symptom: irritability. "Don't grumble against each other, brothers, or you will be judged. The Judge is standing at the door!" (James 5:9).

Rx: "Give thanks in all circumstances, for this is God's will for you in Christ Jesus" (1 Thessalonians 5:18).

Self-examination:

Symptom: being argumentative. "He who is not with me is against me, and he who does not gather with me, scatters" (Luke 11:23).

Rx: "Therefore, I urge you, brothers, in view of God's mercy, to offer your bodies as living sacrifices, holy and pleasing to God—this is your spiritual act of worship" (Romans 12:1).

Self-examination:

Symptom: hearing loss. "See, I am setting before you today a blessing and a curse—the blessing if you obey the commands of the LORD your God that I am giving you today; the curse if you disobey the commands of the LORD your God and turn from the way that I command you today by following other gods, which you have not known" (Deuteronomy 11:26-28).

Rx: "My son, if you accept my words and store up my commands within you, turning your ear to wisdom and applying your heart to understanding, and if you call out for insight and cry aloud for understanding, and if you look for it as for silver and search for it as for hidden treasure, then you will understand the fear of the LORD and find the knowledge of God" (Proverbs 2:1-5).

Self-examination:

Symptom: "big head" syndrome. "Pride goes before destruction, a haughty spirit before a fall" (Proverbs 16:18).

Rx: "Humble yourselves before the Lord, and he will lift you up" (James 4:10).

Self-examination:

Symptom: memory loss. "Be careful that you do not forget the LORD your God, failing to observe his commands, his laws and his decrees that I am giving you this day. . . . Then your heart will become proud and you will forget the LORD your God, who brought you out of Egypt, out of the land of slavery" (Deuteronomy 8:11, 14).

Rx: "We will not hide them from their children; we will tell the next generation the praiseworthy deeds of the LORD, his power, and the wonders he has done" (Psalm 78:4).

Self-examination:

2. Spend time in prayer. Ask God to show you possible sin symptoms you are displaying in your life. Meditate on the verses relating to those symptoms. If there is a specific thing God is asking you to do or change, write it out in the space provided. Ask a friend to hold you accountable in this area. Who will it be, and when will you talk with him or her? Write your plan here also.

OBSCURE
Bible Facts

Ever want to know the price of a Levite? In Numbers 3:11-13, we are told why the Levites were set apart by God: "I have taken the Levites from among the Israelites in place of the first male offspring of every Israelite woman. The Levites are mine, for all the firstborn are mine. When I struck down all the firstborn in Egypt, I set apart for myself every firstborn in Israel, whether man or animal. They are to be mine. I am the LORD." So each firstborn of the Israelites was redeemed by the life (in service) of a Levite. But there were more Israelite firstborn males than Levites—273 more in fact. For these extra 273, Moses was to collect 5 shekels for each one. Thus one Levite's life of service equals 5 shekels equals one redeemed firstborn male.

DAY FIVE: REMEMBER
Follow-Up Appointment

It is important to follow up with your doctor when he has prescribed a specific treatment or therapy. Today we want to follow up with some of the things that have been prescribed throughout the week.

1. We have studied a variety of Scriptures this week. Some might be more pertinent to your current situation than others and might have resonated with you. Find at least one verse that has spoken to you. Write it out. Memorize it. Plan to say it out loud to a friend or family member, explaining why you chose it.

2. Begin a list or chart called "What I've Learned About God." Include the Scripture references that support your insights. (Pages for this purpose are included at the end of this book, but you may want to make your own.)

KORAH & COMPANY: A REBELLIOUS BROOD 🔭 49

3. Praise and thanksgiving can squelch a rebellious attitude. Write down one thing that happened this week that you can praise or thank God for.

4. Plan to share that story with someone. Who will it be, and when will you talk with him or her? Write your plan here.

The Lord Who Heals

In *The Tale of the Tardy Oxcart,* Charles Swindoll included this story: "A father had a rather strong-willed son. On the way to the store he kept telling the child, 'Sit down and buckle the seat belt.' But the little kid just kept standing in the seat. Again he said, 'Sit down and buckle the seat belt.' And after a time or two more, the boy was convinced he had better sit down or disaster would strike. So he slipped down onto the seat, snapped the seat belt closed, and said, 'Daddy, I'm sitting down on the outside, but I'm still standing up on the inside.'"[10]

Have you ever felt like that little boy? I have too. And it's because we all have been infected with this malady called sin. The prophet Isaiah said, "We *all,* like sheep, have gone astray, each of us has turned to *his own* way." Our own way. Not God's way. But praise be to God, because he has provided a remedy, a treatment for this disease! "And the LORD has laid on him the iniquity of us all" (Isaiah 53:6, emphasis added).

God is our ultimate healer. He is Jehovah-rapha, "the LORD who heals" (Exodus 15:26). And he healed us through his Son Jesus Christ. The apostle Peter says it like this: "He himself bore our sins in his body on the tree, so that we might die to sins and live for righteousness; by his wounds you have been healed" (1 Peter 2:24).

He has provided us with the cure for our sin sickness. The treatment is available and free to all. The question that needs to be posed now is, Will you accept the treatment?

OBSCURE OBSERVATIONS

CHAPTER TWO

Like ripples on a tranquil pond / That reach the farthest shore,
Our sins affect those close to us, / And many, many more. —Anonymous

achan:
a man with a secret

STOPPING THE RIPPLE EFFECT OF SIN • JOSHUA 7

No One Will Notice

His name was Theo. He was handsome, with golden fur and a pink, twitchy nose. After months of begging, pleading, and groveling for yet another family pet, I guess I wore my mom down. I remember being shocked when she finally relented and said yes.

Our family was notorious for having bad pet experiences.

For instance, my brother's fish.

My brother received an enormous aquatic tank for Christmas one year and decided to fill it with exotic fish. All went well until we went on vacation. We put one of those dissolving food pellets at the bottom of the tank, hoping it would last the advertised seven days. The pellet did exactly as it was supposed to, but our marine buddies decided they liked the taste of the angelfish more. Poor thing! When we came home, he was hopelessly swimming in circles because all but one little side fin had been devoured during our week away.

Then there was the stray dog my sister and I named Charlie. Evidently he had a severe case of intestinal worms, and you can guess that Mom wasn't thrilled with the outcome of that!

The sweet cat we found on the street did a number on Mom's curtains. He didn't last long.

And our first hamster, thought to be a boy, turned out to be a girl. We discovered this when "he" had babies and subsequently ate them. Yuck!

I was in junior high when we got Theo, an amazingly talented hamster. I should have named him Houdini, because he could escape from any cage, tunnel, or ball. No matter how secure the device, Theo could find a way out, but he wasn't too good at hiding. We usually could find him promptly and return him to his home, which we would then try to make more secure to prevent future breakouts. After this happened several times, when Theo went missing again I didn't worry too much about it and didn't even tell my mom.

But the last time Theo escaped, he caused some problems.

A week had passed since I had seen Theo, and I began to fret a bit, but Mom and Dad still didn't know he was not in his "secure" home. Then the weather turned. A cold front came through, and Dad decided we should turn on the heat, for the first time that season.

Our church was having a revival, and our family was hosting some of the guest speakers and singers at our home. As the furnace kicked on and pumped warm air throughout the house, an unusual smell began to permeate each room. Trying to be polite, our guests didn't say anything . . . until my dad began to wretch, running through the house dry heaving—the odor was that of rotten flesh! A chain reaction developed; everyone ran outside to get some fresh, albeit cold, air. Mom turned off the furnace and opened every window in the house. Such hospitality!

I thought it wise then to share the news that Theo had been missing for over a week. We decided that he had found a better hiding place this time.

Dad reentered the house with a mission: find the dead, rotting hamster. With mirrors and a flashlight in hand, he went into the basement, gagging all the way. Using his tools he found Theo, dead and bloated, in one of the vents. Encasing him in an empty whipped cream container, he promptly gave Theo his rightful burial . . . in the *outdoor* trash can.

After the ordeal was over, Mom and Dad looked at me with a parental glare.

"What?" I said. "I didn't think anyone would notice!"

Oftentimes, we *don't* think anyone will notice. We think we can fly below the radar. Our bad choices, we believe, won't have much impact, especially on those around us. An obscure Bible character named Achan shows us that above or below the radar, our choices do have an impact—a ripple effect. Sinful behavior can reach farther than you ever thought possible.

OBSCURE
Bible Facts

Joshua put a curse on whomever would rebuild the city of Jericho (Joshua 6:26). Several hundred years later, Hiel experienced the effects of that curse and lost both his oldest and youngest sons when he laid Jericho's foundations and set up its gates (1 Kings 16:34).

DAY ONE: READ
Your Sin Will Find You Out

1. As we begin this week's study, let's spend time reading the account of Achan found in Joshua 7. Based on your reading, answer the following questions:

What happened at Ai?

Why did it happen?

What did God say was going to happen because of the sin?

What did God tell Joshua to do?

Describe Achan's actions (v. 21).

What did Joshua and the Israelites do to Achan?

List all those affected by Achan's sin.

2. This incident seems incredibly unfair upon first reading. To give us more understanding, let's investigate the background a little more. Joshua was the commander of Israel after Moses died. His role was to lead the Israelites into the promised land of Canaan to take possession of it (Joshua 1:1-6). God gave certain instructions regarding this process. Read the following directives and write what God required of the Israelites. Include the reasons why, if the passage provides those.

Exodus 23:27-33

Deuteronomy 9:5

Deuteronomy 12:29-31

Deuteronomy 20:16-18

Joshua 6:17-19 (directives for taking the city of Jericho, the first city to be conquered in the promised land)

It is important that we understand the phrase from Joshua 6:17, in which we are told that Jericho and everything in it was supposed to be "devoted to the Lord." Interestingly, the *New American Standard Bible* translates this phrase as "under the ban." The Hebrew word is *cherem*, "a doomed object . . . dedicated thing, things which should have been utterly destroyed."[11] To follow completely God's directives regarding Jericho, the Israelites were to utterly destroy the city and its inhabitants and to place the precious metals found throughout the city in the temple treasury, thus dedicating them to the Lord.

Sin in the Camp

The time had come! The Israelites had been waiting for the day when they could claim their gift. The promise made by God to Abraham nearly seven hundred years earlier finally would be fulfilled. The people of Israel, Abraham's descendants, were about to go into the promised land. This vagabond nation would finally have a place to call home, a homeland that would be theirs forever, after enduring four hundred years of bondage in Egypt and forty years of wandering in the wilderness. It had seemed this day would never arrive.

But God is faithful. He used Moses to deliver his people from slavery and prepare them to enter the land. He commissioned Joshua to be their leader in the conquest of that land. He gave the people an incredible victory over Jericho, the first city they needed to conquer. Because they obeyed God and marched and shouted on cue, the Israelites watched the protective wall around Jericho fall to ruin. The Israelites had made their mark. God had faithfully led in victory.

There were directives, though. Nothing and no one, save Rahab and her family, was to be spared. Jericho was *devoted* to destruction. The city was *under the ban*. No one could profit from this victory. It was a city dedicated wholly to the Lord, and that which was devoted to the Lord was considered holy. Set apart. Untouchable.

Now this conquering thing didn't seem so difficult! Next city on the agenda—Ai, a little town not far from Jericho. After spying out this enemy, Joshua's men determined that only a few of the Israelites would be needed in the battle. It would be an easy victory. Following their advice, Joshua sent merely three thousand soldiers, only to have them flee for their lives from the men of Ai. Besides being humiliated by running away from this pathetic enemy, the Israelites lost thirty-six men.

Joshua couldn't believe the outcome! What in the world had happened? God so faithfully brought implausible victory against Jericho when all the odds were stacked against them. Now, against a small, impossible-to-lose-to foe, Israel was defeated? "God, why?"

We learn through the course of Joshua 7 the reason for God's absence at the battle of Ai—sin. Sin in the camp.

········ ●◖◗● ········

DAY TWO: RELATE
Sin's Lure

This story has many life lessons to consider, and I pray your eyes are being opened to the wonderful things in God's Word as you study (Psalm 119:18). Let's see what we can learn specifically about the lure of sin.

1. On Day One, you identified Achan's actions in Joshua 7:21. List those actions again.

Read Genesis 3:6, from the account of the fall of man, noting Eve's actions. How do the stories compare?

2. Let's dig a little deeper. The word *coveted* is used in Joshua 7:21. This word seems to be at the heart of Achan's troubles. But what does it mean? To find out, we need to do a word study.

·······●● Word Study ●●·········

A word study is a deeper look at the meaning of a word as it has been translated from its original language. In the Old Testament, we will look at the original Hebrew. In the New Testament, it will be the Greek. If you have never done a word study before, that's OK. We'll walk through the process together. Here are the basic steps:

a. From the verse you are reading, select a word you wish to study further.

b. Using a lexicon, find the definition of this word as it was used in its original language. Consider other forms of the word.

c. Using a concordance, find other uses of the word, or variations of the word, in other Bible verses. Compare the uses of the word and consider the context in which it is used in each case.

To perform a word study, you'll need some tools:

- A *Strong's Concordance*—an alphabetical listing with corresponding Scripture references of all the words in the Bible.

- A *lexicon* to the Old and New Testament—a dictionary of Hebrew and/or Greek words.

Don't worry if your personal library doesn't include these books, because you have access to them at your fingertips via the Internet! (If you prefer printed books rather than the computer versions, your church library or Bible bookstore should be able to provide you with what you need.) Several Web sites, including the following, offer the Bible study tools we need:

- www.blueletterbible.org

- www.netbible.org

- www.studylight.com

- www.biblestudytools.com

These sites all work in slightly different ways, but the basic steps to doing a word study remain the same.

For our word study of *coveted*, my preference is the Blue Letter Bible site. Let's look at that site together. On the main page of the Web site, find the section titled "Bible/Dictionary Search." Type "Joshua 7:21" in the space provided. Choose the Bible version you prefer. In this case, I'm using the *NIV (New International Version)*. Click on the "Search" button.

The verses in Joshua 7 will come up, with several blue boxes to the left of each verse. Click on the *C* box next to Joshua 7:21. (The *C* stands for "Concordance and Hebrew/Greek Lexicon.")

Scroll down past the Hebrew text box that comes up and find the phrase with the word *coveted*. Listed next to that phrase is the *Strong's Concordance* number for the word. It is #2530. Also listed is the Hebrew word for *coveted*, which is *chamad*. Click on the Strong's number.

The lexicon results should come up on the next screen. Included will be the English *transliteration* (the Hebrew word written in English letters), the Hebrew pronunciation, and the Bible usage (definition), among other things. You should see this definition of the verb:

> 1) To desire, covet, take pleasure in, delight in
> a) (Qal) to desire
> b) (Niphal) to be desirable
> c) (Piel) to delight greatly, desire[12]

Now let's take it a step further. Scroll down until you come to "Concordance Results." These are all the other verses in the Bible that contain this same Hebrew word. You'll notice the Genesis 3:6 passage is one of them.

Click on "Gen 3:6," and the verse will show up. Go through the same steps we followed for Joshua 7:21. You will find the Hebrew word *chamad* (#2530) again.

Knowing that the word for *covet* is used in both stories, can you see an even stronger correlation between Eve and Achan? Explain.

3. You are probably familiar with a famous passage regarding coveting, found in Exodus 20:17. What does that verse say?

●● Word Study ●● Check to see if this use of *covet* is the same Hebrew word as that found in the Joshua and Genesis passages.

4. Look at the following passage of Scripture; then complete the suggested exercises that follow:

> When tempted, no one should say, "God is tempting me." For God cannot be tempted by evil, nor does he tempt anyone; but each one is tempted when, by his own evil desire, he is dragged away and enticed. Then, after desire has conceived, it gives birth to sin; and sin, when it is full-grown, gives birth to death. (James 1:13-15)

Describe or diagram the path of sin.

●● Word Study ●● Do a Greek word study on *desire* (Strong's #1939—*lust*) as found in James 1:14. (Go through the same process as you did for *coveted*.)

Look back at Genesis 3:6 and Joshua 7:21. How do Eve's and Achan's actions follow the pattern James describes?

5. Joshua felt devastated by Israel's defeat at Ai. He didn't understand the cause of the defeat, so God spelled it out for him . . . S-I-N. God went on to explain the effects of the sin. List the details of both—causes and effects—from Joshua 7:11-13.

Directives

"AAAAAAHH!" The earsplitting battle cry of the Israelite army—six hundred thousand strong—coupled with the collapse of miles of massive earthen walls. *KA-BOOM! CRACK! CRASH!* Achan had never heard such a sound before. *So much for the city of Jericho,* he mused. *It's ours now!*

He and his comrades ran into the midst of the rubble, unable to see clearly through the smoke and dust. Achan remembered the directives given by his commander: "Do not leave anything alive that breathes. Completely destroy them!" So he went about his mission. He didn't relish the gruesome task. The thoughts of Joshua's orders continued to play in his mind. "Spare only Rahab and her family. Don't take anything for yourselves! Do you hear me? Nothing is to be ours. It all belongs to the Lord!"

Just then, amid the mayhem surrounding him and despite the limited visibility, Achan saw something glimmer—a shiny metal. Drawn by curiosity as well as his desire to escape the chaos, he stumbled over the remains of the mud-and-brick home that once stood strong. Encased in its own tomb was an astonishing find. Gold! Lots of it! And silver too! Even with all the ashes and dust, the pile of "rubble" glistened and gleamed as if it had recently been polished. It was beautiful, and worth a fortune! This must have been the home of one of the richest men in Jericho! Well, he wouldn't be around to enjoy it anymore. Not after today.

In his mind, Achan began to struggle. *We're supposed to just leave this here? That's the directive. But why? I don't get it! It's valuable! You know how many herds I could buy with this?*

"Don't take anything!" The memory of the voice of his commander interrupted his thoughts.

I know, I know. But what's one bar of gold going to hurt? I won't take it all. I can't—it's too heavy. Just this one bar. He picked it up and hid it in his garment. He turned to go, but the thought of leaving the silver behind made him crazy. He could fit at least of few of the coins in his belt. *No one will notice.* So he grabbed several shekels of silver and carefully placed them where no one would see.

He started to run, knowing he needed to return to the task at hand, when something else caught his eye. A robe . . . and an exquisite one too. It looked as though it could have hung in the wardrobe of a king! With great care Achan concealed the intricately woven fabric with his other finds.

Well into the night, Achan returned to his tent. His body ached all over, but the soreness would subside. It was worth it. A tinge of guilt seared his conscience as he removed the spoils of his day's work. "Don't take anything!" seemed to ring a little louder in his head than it had earlier in the day. Maybe he shouldn't let anyone see his treasures just yet. He began to dig a hole under his tent, a hole big enough to accommodate the booty.

That'll do, he thought. *No one will notice . . .*

DAY THREE: RELATE
Sin's Cure

The situation could have seemed hopeless. God said he would not be with the Israelites anymore, and without God they couldn't win against their enemies! Yet all was not lost, because God gave them a way back.

1. Read Joshua 7:11-15 and outline God's plan to restore Israel.

2. Look up the following passages. How do they relate to Achan and Israel?

Matthew 5:29, 30; 18:7-9

Galatians 5:9

3. Achan sinned and paid the price for that sin. Let's see how we compare. Look up the following verses; then describe our condition and, if stated, the price paid because of that condition:

Isaiah 53:6

Isaiah 59:2

Romans 3:9, 23

Romans 5:8, 9

Romans 5:18, 19

Romans 6:23

4. Although sin has a cure, it also leaves a legacy. Think of a rock thrown into a pond. The rock hitting the water takes only an instant, but we can see the effects for a while afterward. Sin has a ripple effect too. Sin will take you farther than you ever thought you'd stray, keep you longer than you ever thought you'd stay, and cost you more than you ever thought you'd pay.

What price did Achan end up paying for his sin?

Who else was affected by his actions?

What does Numbers 14:18 say about the sin of the fathers affecting the generations that follow?

5. The following verses show a distinct difference in the life of one who follows God completely versus one who seeks his own way. Chart the contrasts you see.

Scripture	Those Who Keep God's Commands	Those Who Don't
Deuteronomy 7:9, 10		
1 Corinthians 6:9-11		
Colossians 3:3-17		

Called Out

"Achan! Achan! Come quickly!" Achan's wife shouted in a flurry. "Joshua has called a meeting—and he wants *everyone* there!"

Achan got up from his bed.

"Hurry, Achan! This must be important. Maybe he's revamping the strategy for the upcoming battle, seeing how our men failed so miserably at Ai."

Achan followed his wife as she gathered all the children and tried to hurry them along the crowded path to where Joshua would speak. All Israel had turned out. Achan stood near the back with his family. If there was something vital to know about, odds are they would find it out. Nothing stayed hidden with this group!

"The tribe of Judah!" came the shouts. "Anyone in the tribe of Judah needs to move forward!"

"Achan!" his wife yelled. "That's us! Come, we must make our way."

Something didn't feel right. Achan walked reluctantly toward the place where Joshua stood.

"The family of Zerah!"

"Did you hear that, Achan? That's us too! What is this about? Is this to honor someone for his service?"

Achan began to feel uneasy. Honor someone . . . or call them out? He prayed it wasn't the latter.

One by one the men of Zerah came before Joshua. Achan managed to avoid looking directly into Joshua's eyes. He felt uncomfortable and not partial to being in a lineup. He willed Joshua to pick someone else . . . anyone else . . . and let him out of there!

Joshua tagged Zabdi, Achan's grandfather.

What was going on? Surely this had to do with someone other than Achan. Was it the gold? No one knew about the gold! He had hidden it! Had someone seen him hide it? He'd been so careful to keep everything hidden. He—

"Achan. Come forward." Joshua's order jolted Achan from his frenzied thoughts. Sweat trickled from his forehead.

Joshua stood face-to-face with Achan, and the entire nation of Israel looked on. "My son," Joshua began.

Was Joshua addressing him? He knew! Somehow he knew!

"Give glory to the Lord, the God of Israel, and give him the praise."

That was it! He was done in! It wasn't a lot, really. Just one bar of gold! A little silver too, but that's not much! Who told Joshua? How did he find out? What was going to happen to Achan now?

"Tell me what you have done," Joshua continued, "Do not hide it from me."

Achan's guilt pierced his heart. "It's true!" he cried out. "I have sinned against the Lord, the God of Israel."

The crowd gasped. Achan's wife clung to her children, who all stood silent, stunned at the turn of events. Whatever Achan had done, she knew severe consequences would follow. She looked into the innocent faces of her little ones. What would become of them?

Before she knew it, a group of messengers was being sent to their tent. What were they looking for? What was this about? Panic swelled within her. *Achan! What have you done?*

The messengers returned with the stolen articles and spread them before Joshua and all the people in the sight of the Lord God. Suddenly a mob descended on Achan's wife. Hands pulled at her hair, arms lifted her from the ground. "No! Stop!" She saw her children being carried away. "Let them go! Let them go!" she screamed. "Achan! You fool! Look what you have done!"

The throng slowed its pace near the Valley of Achor and threw down Achan and his stolen articles. They tossed his wife and children next to him, and then his sheep and donkeys.

As Achan's wife tried to make sense of things, she heard Joshua's voice above the fray, his words directed toward Achan: "Why have you brought this trouble on us? The Lord will bring trouble on you today."

And before she could formulate another thought, Achan's wife felt the impact of huge stones hurled at her. They pummeled her back, her arms, and her head. Her ears began to ring, and the light began to fade. She looked up and met Achan's gaze.

With blood trickling from his mouth and down his head, he cried out, "I'm sorry! I'm so sorry." Then everything went black.

OBSCURE
Bible Facts

The Valley of Achor (*akowr*, 5911) can accurately be translated the Valley of Trouble. This is where Achan, the troubler of Israel (Joshua 7:25), was stoned. Both Isaiah and Hosea would later use the phrase "valley of trouble" as a way of illustrating God's redemption of Israel (Isaiah 65:10; Hosea 2:15).

DAY FOUR: REFLECT
Under the Ban

Like Achan, we all have desired and longed for things that God has placed "under the ban" (Joshua 6:17, 18, *NASB*). Maybe we feel the things under the ban are placed there unfairly. But we've seen that God has good reasons for the boundaries he sets.

1. What is one thing you find alluring or desirable that might be considered under the ban or off limits?

At what point do desires become covetous?

Is allowing a little bit of an off-limit desire in your life all right? Why or why not?

If you have gone for something under the ban, what was it or what is it?

Why would God place it under the ban?

How has your family been affected? your work? your church? your community?

What does God require to restore you (or what did he require)?

Sometimes we are blind to the sin in our life. Ask God to open your eyes to the things you've allowed in your life that are under the ban. Once he reveals these to you, seek his wisdom in how to remove and destroy them.

2. So many times we hone in on only the negative and neglect to celebrate the victories God gives. Once Joshua and the Israelites removed and destroyed the things under the ban, they again faced the enemy at Ai. This time God gave them great victory *and* the spoils of war!

   Is there a time you can recount in which your obedience to God resulted in reward?

   Who else was affected through this situation?

   The Israelites worshipped God after their great victory. Spend time worshipping and praising him for his goodness, faithfulness, and provision in your life.

DAY FIVE: REMEMBER
Axioms

Axioms are short, pithy statements that give guidelines to live by and lessons to learn from. These clever little sayings can instill wisdom without being overbearing.

The teachings in the Bible have given us many familiar axioms:

- "Pride goes before destruction" (Proverbs 16:18).

- Do unto others as you would have them do unto you (from Matthew 7:12).

- Love the Lord your God with all your heart, soul, mind, and strength (from Deuteronomy 6:5 and Matthew 22:37).

- "Love your neighbor as yourself" (Matthew 22:39).

- You reap what you sow (from Galatians 6:7).

- Humble yourself before the Lord, and he will lift you up (from James 4:10).

1. Choose a verse that spoke to you this week. Work on committing this verse to memory. Review the verse you memorized last week.

2. What did you learn about God this week? Continue to add to your list or chart.

Achan's Axioms

In his book *Axiom*, Bill Hybels encourages leaders to "pinpoint their guiding principles on the important stuff of leadership and distill them down to memorable sound-bites that can be called upon at a second's notice."[13] My husband, always a fan of leadership techniques, grabbed onto Hybels's strategy. Actually, Ron realized he's been instilling axioms in our family for years, but now he had a name for it! And if you ask my kids what some of their dad's favorite phrases are, they will promptly respond "Blackmores don't lie," "Be on time," and (one of *my* favorites) "Make Momma happy!"

To bring this week's lesson to its conclusion, let's take a closer look at some pithy axioms plucked specifically from Achan's story.

If It Gets in the Way of Obedience, Get Rid of It

Of all the axioms introduced to our family, this has been one of the hardest to swallow.

Books, activities, relationships, movies, and TV shows have all been scrutinized and analyzed using this axiom. I can't tell you the number of beloved toys, CDs, and video games tossed from our household, usually with many tears.

The end results have been worth the drama. And not only have we applied this axiom to our children, but Ron and I have had to implement it in our own lives on several occasions. Matthew 5:29, 30 says, "If your right eye causes you to sin, gouge it out and throw it away. It is better for you to lose one part of your body than for your whole body to be thrown into hell. And if your right hand causes you to sin, cut it off and throw it away. It is better for you to lose one part of your body than for your whole body to go into hell."

Pretty straightforward, wouldn't you say? Other verses that speak to this, but in a manner a bit more subtle, come from Matthew 6:22, 23: "The eye is the lamp of the body. If your eyes are good, your whole body will be full of light. But if your eyes are bad, your whole body will be full of darkness." For years these verses made no sense to me, until one day I recognized that our eyes help us focus.

Let me explain.

My first job out of college was selling insurance door to door. Taking this job wasn't the wisest decision I've ever made, trust me. My husband and I had been married one week when I accepted this position. I promptly had to leave him for the next three weeks for out-of-town training to get my insurance license. Not the best way for newlyweds to spend their first days as a married couple!

Armed with my license and a new set of selling skills, I went with excitement to my first sales meeting, where the director repeatedly shared how to achieve success—the ultimate goal. Not success helping people purchase the best policy for their needs but success measured in the amount of money you made and the number of things you could buy with it.

The director told us to go home that day and cut out magazine pictures of things we desired to have . . . a big home, a fancy new car, a lavish swimming pool. He suggested we put those pictures on our refrigerator and look at them every day. *Focus* on them, he said. He guaranteed that in time we would have those very things.

He himself had experienced the power of images. One of the pictures he placed on his fridge was that of a huge house. Eventually, he said, that house was realized, and he went out and bought a beautiful new riding lawn mower too. He didn't really need a riding mower, so he wondered why he bought more than what was necessary. Then one day as he was inspecting his fridge pic more carefully, he noticed a fancy riding lawn mower in the background, just like the one he had recently purchased!

Whether all this was true or a ploy to get our team motivated, the lesson behind it hit me hard: the things we focus on impact our decisions.

Achan focused on what allured him. Rather than running, he kept gazing. Eventually that led to a decision that negatively impacted him, his family, and his nation. God's directive to remove the sin was harsh, hurtful, far-reaching, and effective. If sin had been left in the camp, the Israelites would never have been able to stand against their enemies. They would never have been able to claim their inheritance. Even more important, God would not have been with them. As we learned earlier, God's presence with the Israelites when they faced their enemies was tied to their obedience.

Many things in this world allure and entice. They seem to call out to us. We allow ourselves to focus on the things that take our eyes off Christ. We rationalize and justify and eventually allow sin to settle into our lives. Don't do it! Follow this important axiom instead. If sin is in your camp, remove it. And do it quickly.

Your Sin Will Find You Out

A story has been told about a little boy who stole his sister's favorite doll. Not wanting anyone to find out, he buried the doll in the backyard. When questioned by his mother, the boy adamantly denied he had taken it. Thinking his sin would never be discovered, the boy carried on as if he were completely innocent. All went according to plan until springtime, when a patch of flowers erupted in the backyard—in the shape of a rag doll! The doll was made of fabric and stuffed with seeds. The boy quickly learned his sin would indeed find him out.

Hiding—it's a huge red flag, a neon sign indicating something isn't right. Did you notice this behavioral pattern with both Achan and Eve when they knew they had done something against God's plan? They hid. Achan hid the stolen articles under his tent. Eve hid herself, trying to dodge the eyes of God. I remember doing the very same thing as a child whenever I did something I knew would be displeasing to my parents. And I'm not proud to admit it, but even as an adult I've hidden things I knew would be displeasing to friends and family.

Can you relate? I'd venture to guess that most people probably can. Isn't it odd that we seem more concerned with what everyone else might think rather than what God thinks? *Nothing* is hidden from his sight.

We should view hiding as a banner with "DANGER" in big block letters. For when we try to hide what we've done, we fool ourselves and inevitably get ourselves and others into trouble. Consider these verses:

. . . .

[The wicked] say, "The Lord does not see; the God of Jacob pays no heed." (Psalm 94:7)

Woe to those who go to great depths to hide their plans from the Lord, who do their work in darkness and think, "Who sees us? Who will know?" (Isaiah 29:15)

Everything that is hidden will eventually be brought into the open, and every secret will be brought to light. (Mark 4:22, *NLT*)

. . . .

One of the Hebrew names of God is *Elroi,* the God who sees. This name is extremely revealing of God's character, for he sees all. Nothing escapes his attention; his vision is vast and penetrates deeply. "From heaven the LORD looks down and sees all mankind; from his dwelling place he watches all who live on earth—he who forms the hearts of all, who considers everything they do" (Psalm 33:13-15). "The LORD does not look at the things man looks at. Man looks at the outward appearance, but the LORD looks at the heart" (1 Samuel 16:7). We may talk ourselves into believing we can hide things from other people, but the one who matters can see all. Nothing escapes his view.

So what are you hiding? What have you been keeping secret? Be aware that it won't remain a secret, no matter how hard you try or how secure the secret seems. Your sins will find you out.

There's No Such Thing as Partial Obedience

Have you ever heard of a husband or wife who was 90 percent faithful to his or her marriage? Ludicrous, right? You're either faithful to your partner or not. Or what about a freshly cleaned shirt? One tiny stain shouldn't ruin the whole article, should it? I don't know about you, but if my white shirt has even a small mark I can't get out, I'm ready to toss it away.

Achan was the small mark on Israel's white shirt. Even though everyone else followed God's orders completely, Achan did not. His sin tarnished God's people. (You've heard about one bad apple spoiling the whole bunch?) God said: "*Israel* has sinned; *they* have violated my covenant, which I commanded them to keep. *They* have taken some of the devoted things; *they* have stolen, *they* have lied, *they* have put them with their own possessions" (Joshua 7:11, emphasis added). The end result was that God was not with Israel, at least not while the stain was still there.

Once the Israelites removed the stain (aka Achan), they set out to follow God completely, and God honored their obedience. Joshua 8 chronicles the second attempt to take Ai. God gave specific instructions, and Joshua and the people of Israel carried out those instructions perfectly. Ai was destroyed, and not a single man of Israel was lost in the battle. Joshua then took time to read God's law, every word of it, to the whole assembly—men, women, and children as well as the foreigners living among them. God and his laws guided them and his words were to be adhered to completely.

We are God's people. We are his ambassadors. When we sin, God's reputation is at stake. Partially following his commands compromises his glory. Partially following his commands is not really following his commands at all. Because there's no such thing as partial obedience.

One Last Thought

When I first read Achan's story, I felt uncomfortable with the punishment doled out to him and his family. Maybe you did too. Perhaps it was because I could relate to Achan and his desires, or because I know I too have sinned and will sin again. Maybe I like viewing God as one who loves, not one who punishes. But the more I thought about this, prayed through it, and studied the Word, the more I have come to appreciate the lesson of Achan and the God who loved his people enough to cut out the cancer. (What an incredibly difficult thing to do!)

I still have some issues to settle, though. Issues such as . . .

- *I am a sinner.* But God knows that . . . and took my sin from me so I could be made right with God (2 Corinthians 5:21).

- *I lose my way on occasion.* But God knows that . . . he gave me his Spirit to live in me, guide me, and empower me (1 Corinthians 6:19; John 16:13, Acts 1:8).

- *I need second chances.* But God knows that . . . so he gave me a way back through confession and repentance (1 John 1:9, Luke 24:47).

Achan's story, stripped to its bare bones, is a story about grace. And when I think of God's grace toward me, a sinner like Achan, my response is a deep and abounding gratitude. My prayer is that his grace in my life doesn't just ripple out to those around me but becomes a tidal wave—a tsunami of salvation.

OBSCURE OBSERVATIONS

The great use of life is to spend it for something that will outlast it.
—William James

deborah and jael:
a career-driven woman and a stay-at-home mom

UNDERSTANDING YOUR VALUE • JUDGES 4, 5

I Was Born to . . .

"It was the best of times, it was the worst of times."[14] Although Charles Dickens penned these words about the French Revolution (in *A Tale of Two Cities*), he could have been referring to biblical times as well. The nation of Israel had just experienced an extended period of great victory by conquering the promised land of Canaan. God then raised up individuals to lead the various Israelite tribes and empowered them to serve as judges, yet the time of the judges was also a 340-year downward spiral into moral bankruptcy and societal chaos. During this time, tolerance of sin, a departure from God's truths, and moral relativism permeated the land, evidenced by rampant stealing, idolatry, opportunism, sexual brutality, infidelity, and homosexuality (see Judges 17–21). Sounds like today's news, doesn't it?

The moral corruption and pervasive evil made its way to the highways and byways as well. Judges 5 depicts marauders everywhere and unsafe conditions for everyone from travelers to farmers. The people lived in fear that escalated year after year. The dark days of the judges got darker and darker.

That is until Deborah and Jael arose! Judges 4 and 5 capture a story of bright lights in the darkness—two very different women with two very different callings.

Calling. Some people seem to understand their calling in life—their purpose—right from the start. In a funny romantic comedy I watched several years ago, the main character found the man of her dreams and told him, "I was born to love you!" Pretty strong sentiment, especially since she had only met him a few hours prior to this declaration! My dad, a chemist, had chemistry in his blood as an infant, I feel certain. Given the opportunity, I'll bet he would have figured out the formula for his own formula! My husband knew in middle school that he wanted to be a physician. He stayed focused on that goal and worked diligently to receive his medical degree. Early in her high school career, my sister became interested in learning sign language. She got her masters in audiology and now interprets for the deaf. My daughter has her sights set on being a ninth-grade math teacher. Mind you, she's only in the eighth grade right now, but she feels certain she will teach ninth-grade math!

Me? I attended three different colleges, changed my major six times, got a degree in business, economics, and Bible (weird combination, I know), and ended up staying at home with two children. But I believe wholeheartedly that I am fulfilling part of my calling by being the proverbial soccer mom.

Does this mean I would not be fulfilling my calling if I went back to work outside the home? What about other moms who do so or have always been employed? Do their jobs complete their calling?

Several years ago I came across a Scripture that helped me understand that our calling does not necessarily have to be our occupation. Calling reaches beyond that. Daniel 11:32 says, "The people who know their God will display strength and take action" (*NASB*). I find this liberating because it helps me see that the bigger purpose of my life is to know God. He guarantees that when we pursue him, great things will be accomplished through us for his kingdom. This guarantee comes regardless of our station in life and regardless of the circumstances of the world around us. That's exciting!

DAY ONE: READ
The Tale of Two Women

Judges 4 tells us the story in narrative form. Judges 5 is Deborah's song of victory and gives details in a more poetic style. Use both chapters to glean information to answer these questions:

1. Name the major players and their roles.

2. Describe the conditions in Israel. How long did this last?

3. Name the biggest hero in this story, and give a reason for your answer.

4. What methods did God use to route Sisera's army?

5. Compare the two armies. What do you learn from the text about each?

Israel's army:

Sisera's army:

6. Some of the tribes of Israel supported Deborah and Barak; others did not. According to Judges 5:12-18, how did each of the following respond?

Ephraim

Benjamin

Machir

Zebulun

Issachar

Reuben

Gilead

Dan

Asher

Naphtali

Day Two: Read
Setting the Stage

To fully appreciate Deborah and Jael, we need to set the historical stage.

The people of Israel had gotten themselves into a cycle of sin, summarized in Judges 2:11-20. Read the passage; then work through the instructions that follow it.

. . . .

Then the Israelites did evil in the eyes of the Lord and served the Baals. They forsook the Lord, the God of their fathers, who had brought them out of Egypt. They followed and worshipped various gods of the peoples around them. They provoked the Lord to anger because they forsook him and served Baal and the Ashtoreths. In his anger against Israel the Lord handed them over to raiders who plundered them. He sold them to their enemies all around, whom they were no longer able to resist. Whenever Israel went out to fight, the hand of the Lord was against them to defeat them, just as he had sworn to them. They were in great distress.

Then the Lord raised up judges, who saved them out of the hands of these raiders. Yet they would not listen to their judges but prostituted themselves to other gods and worshipped them. Unlike their fathers, they quickly turned from the way in which their fathers had walked, the way of obedience to the Lord's commands. Whenever the Lord raised up a judge for them, he was with the judge and saved them out of the hands of their enemies as long as the judge lived; for the Lord had compassion on them as they groaned under those who oppressed and afflicted them. But when the judge died, the people returned to ways even more corrupt than those of their fathers, following other gods and serving and worshipping them. They refused to give up their evil practices and stubborn ways.

Therefore the LORD was very angry with Israel. (Judges 2:11-20)

. . . .

1. What did Israel do? Underline in red all the action phrases.

2. Underline in blue what God did.

3. Circle in red Israel's emotional responses.

4. Circle in blue God's emotional responses.

5. Fill in the blanks to describe Israel's sin cycle:

   Israel forsook

   _____

   The Lord was provoked to

   _____

   The Lord sold the Israelites to their

   _____

The Lord had compassion on them as they

_____

The Lord raised up

_____

The people refused to give up their

_____

Therefore the Lord was

_____

6. Israel continued to fall into sin for at least two reasons. Look up the following verses and define the problems:

Judges 2:10

Judges 17:6

Putting the Plan in Place

When God called out the nation of Israel as his own and designated the people to be his own possession (Exodus 19:5), he promised them a land they could call their own, the land of Canaan (Genesis 17:8). Over many years, God kept that promise alive by confirming it to Israel's patriarchs and leaders, including Abraham, Isaac, Jacob, and Joseph. And as always, God made good on his promise. He led the Israelites out of captivity in Egypt by the hand of a man named Moses. Although Moses did not have the opportunity to bring the Israelites into the land of promise, the young man he trained—Joshua—did.

The Key to Success

As Joshua took over the leadership of Israel, God made perfectly clear that he would be with Joshua as he had been with Moses. Joshua obeyed God and fulfilled his calling. He honored God with his obedience and trusted him with each battle. The land of Canaan became Israel's land.

Now I want to make note of something here as I'm rattling off nearly a thousand years of history in only a few sentences: Israel's conquest of Canaan was guaranteed— God said it would happen, and it did. However, God's desire and command cannot be overlooked. Success depended on obedience. God told Joshua to meditate on and follow all the law of Moses (Joshua 1:8). *That* would be the key to such success!

Near the end of his life, Joshua reiterated this key to the people of Israel when he said, "You yourselves have seen everything the LORD your God has done to all these nations for your sake; it was the LORD your God who fought for you. . . . Be very strong; be careful to obey all that is written in the Book of the Law of Moses, without turning aside to the right or to the left. . . . But you are to hold fast to the LORD your God, as you have until now" (Joshua 23:3, 6, 8).

So here's a life lesson right off the bat. Follow God's commands and we will prosper; ignore them and we're in trouble.

Sin's Slippery Slope

As soon as Joshua died, everyone in Israel began doing "what was right in his own eyes" (Judges 21:25, *NASB*). Subtle disobedience eventually became blatant. Isn't that the way it goes? Desensitization happens every day in our own world. Think about it. Many current social standards used to be viewed as morally unacceptable. Consider the following facts.

A Media Education Foundation fact sheet reported in 2005: "Research indicates that media violence has not just increased in quantity; it has also become more graphic, sexual, and sadistic."[15]

William Robert Johnston published data in February 2008 showing U.S. abortion rates from 1960–2005. The data show an estimated 292 abortions in 1960 but 1,206,200 in 2005. The percentage of abortions per total number of pregnancies went from .01 percent in 1960 to 22.6 percent in 2005.[16]

In 2000 *Psychology Today* reported 4.2 million cohabitating, unmarried couples living in the United States in 1998 compared to 439,000 in 1963.[17]

Although Lucille Ball and Desi Arnaz, stars of the popular TV show *I Love Lucy* (1951–1957), were married in real life, the show depicted them sleeping in separate twin beds.[18] In that way, any notion of a sexual relationship between the two was held at bay. Today, standards have changed. As entertainment writer Christopher Lyon said, "Any alien culture judging us by our TV and movies would have to conclude that sex is our highest ideal. What else to do we talk about or simulate more often?" Lyon also shared insight on why marriage is no longer a criteria for having sex and not even part of the conversation: "The entertainment industry has without a doubt radicalized our notions of sex. In the 1990s, *Seinfeld* and *Friends* helped us get over the idea that sex among attractive twenty-somethings needed to be burdened by love talk. Most people under forty are now aware of TV's popular three-date rule. And the current sitcom champ *Two and a Half Men* moved us past the decade-old idea that you should wait three dates before having sex. If Charlie Sheen's character waits till the first commercial break, it's a slow episode."[19]

Can you see how far things have fallen?

Did these changes occur overnight? No. We became and continue to be desensitized to these sights, sounds, images, and ideas over time.

This same decline is depicted in Psalm 1. Notice the verbs in the first verse: "Blessed is the man who does not *walk* in the counsel of the wicked or *stand* in the way of sinners or *sit* in the seat of mockers" (Psalm 1:1, emphasis added). The psalmist is showing us the progression of one who gets comfortable with sin. The verbs picture his actions. Initially not interested in what is happening with the wicked, he walks right past. Then he slows down and begins to stand in their path. His comfort level allows him to hang around, so to speak. Eventually, that does not suffice anymore, and he finds himself sitting in the midst of evil, wallowing in it, if you will. He is completely desensitized to the sin that offended him at the outset.

The Israelites experienced this same desensitization. In Judges 1 we read that after Joshua died, the Israelites continued their conquest of the promised land. Initially they drove out its inhabitants as God commanded. They became lax in following the directive, however, and allowed some of their enemies to remain, first as forced laborers. Eventually God's people embraced the culture and religion of these prior adversaries. Ultimately, a new generation arose that did not know God or the works he had done (Judges 2:8-10). God's ways were forgotten; everyone made up his own rules (Judges 17:6; 21:25). But in God's great compassion, he provided a glimmer of hope through Deborah and Jael.

> **OBSCURE**
> **Bible Facts**
>
> There are at least five women in the Old Testament who bore the title prophetess: Miriam, Moses' sister (Exodus 15:20); Deborah (Judges 4:4); Huldah (2 Kings 22:14); Noadiah (Nehemiah 6:14) and the unnamed wife of Isaiah (Isaiah 8:3).

DAY THREE: RELATE
Two Women, Two Callings

Let's spend some time learning more about Deborah and Jael and the other players in their story in Judges 4, 5.

1. What specific descriptions are given about Deborah?

What command(s) did she give Barak?

How did she know to summon Barak?

How did she respond when Jael killed the enemy?

What character traits does she demonstrate? Give examples.

2. What was Barak's initial response to Deborah's command?

What is your gut reaction to that?

Read Hebrews 11:32, 33. Does this change or support your opinion of Barak? Why?

3. To what people group did Jael belong?

Read the following cross-references about the Kenites. What was their relationship with Israel? Judges 1:16

Numbers 10:29-34

Why did Sisera flee to Jael's tent?

How did Deborah describe Jael?

What character traits did she demonstrate?

4. What did God do for Israel in this battle?

Whom did God use to accomplish his goals? Why is this significant?

Displaying Strength and Taking Action

As long as we are pursuing our God to know him, we can do great things for him—whether we are leading a nation or kissing a boo-boo! Deborah, a working woman, and Jael, a woman "in the tent" (Judges 5:24, *NASB*)—a stay-at-home mom—each understood her own role, but even more important is that each had a principal calling to know God. As a result both women were able to "display strength and take action" (Daniel 11:32, *NASB*).

Deborah, a Career-Driven Woman

Read Judges 4:1-4 again, where the setting is given for Deborah's arrival: "After Ehud died, the Israelites once again did evil in the eyes of the LORD. So the LORD sold them into the hands of Jabin, a king of Canaan, who reigned in Hazor. The commander of his army was Sisera, who lived in Harosheth Haggoyim. Because he had nine hundred iron chariots and had cruelly oppressed the Israelites for twenty years, they cried to the LORD for help. Deborah, a prophetess, the wife of Lappidoth, was leading Israel at that time."

Do you see the cycle? Israel did *evil*. God gave the people into the hands of an *enemy*, Jabin and Sisera. The Israelites *cried out*. God appointed Deborah, their *judge*, to rescue them.

I find it odd that God raised up a woman to lead Israel at this time, don't you? Don't misunderstand me. I fully believe women are completely capable of leading and smart beyond measure, but very rarely in biblical accounts do we see women leading a nation.

Scripture does not leave us hanging as to God's reasons for choosing Deborah. Judges 5 is Deborah's victory song, which reveals a possible reason Deborah was the woman of the hour: "In the days of Shamgar son of Anath, in the days of Jael, the roads were abandoned; travelers took to winding paths. Village life in Israel ceased, ceased until I, Deborah, arose, arose a mother in Israel. . . . My heart is with Israel's princes, with the willing volunteers among the people. Praise the LORD!" (Judges 5:6, 7, 9).

We know that God, being *sovereign*, supreme in authority and power, placed Deborah in her position. But we can see from her song that the desperate conditions stirred Deborah's heart. She was compassionate to the cause and passionate for the cause. God used the difficult times and situation to move Deborah to arise.

What about you? What causes, what desperate conditions stir your heart? We're not told of Deborah's qualifications. We don't know her background, personal experience, or level of education. Did she come from money or from the other side of the tracks? Was she short or tall, heavy or skinny? Was she fluent in many languages or did she stutter? We don't know. Why? Because those things don't matter when God stirs your heart for his cause. What matters is that you arise!

Deborah arose. Her heart was stirred. Here was Deborah's opportunity to display strength and take action! We can conclude that she knew God well enough to take this step of faith because she acted on God's command; she summoned Barak with the intention of rallying the troops.

Deborah's confidence in God can be seen in her actions, yet her song gives us the little details that help us understand the depth of her faith in Almighty God. Judges 5:8 says, "Not a shield or spear was seen among forty thousand in Israel." Israel had no weapons! God asked Deborah to lead a war effort without appropriate weaponry against an enemy that had oppressed Israel for twenty years! Look closely at Judges 4:3 and you'll see the reason for the oppression and intimidation; Jabin and Sisera had nine hundred iron chariots! Not only did they have the controlling hand in this relationship emotionally, but they also had a well-equipped, powerful army to back them up. But Deborah seemed undaunted. God commanded Israel to go, and that's what Deborah would do!

Barak's response seems a little less confident. He didn't want to go unless Deborah went with him. We might think, *What a wimp, hiding behind Deborah.* However, maybe we should give Barak a little more credit. He realized that Deborah's confidence couldn't possibly be in Israel's troops; it had to be in something more, something bigger, *someone* bigger! Deborah heard from God; therefore, she must know God. And if she knew God, then God was on her side. Barak's faith, then, could be in God too: "Deborah, I'll go if you go, because I know God is with you." Hebrews 11, the "Hall of Faith" chapter of the Bible, confirms that Barak was a man "who through faith conquered kingdoms" (v. 33).

It's exciting to see the story play out. Deborah and Barak knew God. In that knowledge they were able to arise—to display strength and take action. And the enemy army was completely obliterated! Israel had no weapons, while Sisera had many. What Israel *did* have, however, was a leader who knew God and a powerful God who fought for his people. The Lord was the one who routed Sisera and all his chariots, and he did it with great drama. Deborah sings God's praises and tells us how God fought for Israel:

. . . .

When the princes in Israel take the lead,
  when the people willingly offer themselves—
  praise the Lord!

Hear this, you kings! Listen, you rulers!
  I will sing to the Lord, I will sing;
  I will make music to the Lord, the God of Israel.

O Lord, when you went out from Seir,
  when you marched from the land of Edom,
  the earth shook, the heavens poured,
  the clouds poured down water.

The mountains quaked before the Lord, the One of Sinai,
  before the Lord, the God of Israel.

From the heavens the stars fought,
  from their courses they fought against Sisera.

The river Kishon swept them away,
  the age-old river, the river Kishon.
  March on, my soul; be strong! (Judges 5:2-5, 20, 21)

. . . .

God used a great storm to route the enemy. What happens when large amounts of water rain down from heaven? The earth gets muddy. How well do chariot wheels work in mud? Not too well!

Aren't you thankful God preserved this story of Deborah for us today? Deborah shows us how to arise and follow God's call. First, we need to be sensitive to the stirring of our hearts. God gives each of us different gifts, passions, talents, life experiences, and personality traits. He can use these to stir our hearts and awaken a passion we might not have had previously. Once he kindles that passion in us, he calls us to do something about it . . . to arise! We cannot go it alone, though. Our purpose and calling can only be fully achieved in the knowledge of God. Deborah lived that out and left an example for us to follow.

She knew God.

She displayed strength.

She took action.

Jael, a Stay-at-Home Mom

One of my all-time favorite gifts is a yellow plastic tent peg with "You Go, Girl!" written on it in black ink. My friend Lisa sent it to me after I shared with our Bible study group that one of my heroes is Jael, a woman "in the tent" (Judges 5:24, *NASB*)—in other words, a stay-at-home mom.

Being a stay-at-home mom myself, I felt I could relate to Jael. I'm sure Lisa, also a stay-at-home mom, did too. Lisa and her husband have five children. Her husband teaches at a small private school and makes a modest income. Financial struggles seem to surface often, yet I have never heard Lisa complain about their situation. Contentment is one of her many great qualities. Their family does have options, for Lisa has her doctorate in human development and family studies and could very easily enter the workforce to add to the family income. As a couple, however, Lisa and her husband sought God's plan for their family and decided to have Dr. Lisa remain at home to raise their children.

Lisa has a strong sense that she is called right now to be a stay-at-home mom. I believe I have that same calling. Does this mean our influence in society is limited? Does it mean our role is insignificant and our value diminished? Our world would have us believe such.

Not long ago I heard an interview with retired philosophy professor Linda Hirshman, who made several inflammatory comments regarding women who choose to stay at home with children. I have since read articles in which she said similar derisive things, including, "An educated, competent adult's place is in the office"[20] and "The tasks of housekeeping and child rearing [are] not worthy of the full time and talents of intelligent and educated human beings."[21] She has also expressed that "the family—with its repetitious, socially invisible, physical tasks—is a necessary part of life, but it allows fewer opportunities for full human flourishing than public spheres like the market or the government."[22]

The role of the stay-at-home mom has been undermined for years. I received the following story in an e-mail from a friend:

A woman renewing her driver's license at the county clerk's office was asked by the female recorder to state her occupation. She hesitated, uncertain how to classify herself.

"What I mean is," explained the recorder, "do you have a job or are you just a —?"

"Of course I have a job," snapped the woman. "I'm a mom."

"We don't list *mom* as an occupation. *Housewife* covers it," said the recorder emphatically.

I forgot all about this story until I found myself in the same situation, this time at our own town hall. Poised, efficient, and possessing the high-sounding title of town registrar, the clerk asked, "And what is your occupation?"

What made me say it? I do not know. The words simply popped out: "I'm a research associate in the field of child development and human relations."

The clerk paused, ball-point pen frozen in midair, and looked up as though she had not heard right.

I repeated myself slowly, emphasizing the most significant words. Then I stared with wonder as the clerk wrote my pronouncement in bold black ink on the official questionnaire.

"Might I ask," said the clerk with new interest, "just what you do in your field?"

I heard myself reply coolly, with no trace of fluster in my voice:

"I have a continuing program of research . . ." *What mother doesn't?*

". . . in the laboratory and in the field." *Indoors and out.*

"I'm working for my masters . . ." *First the Lord and then the whole family.*

". . . and I already have four credits." *All daughters.*

"Of course, the job is one of the most demanding in the humanities." *Any mother care to disagree?*

"I often work fourteen hours a day." *Twenty-four is more like it!*

"But the job is more challenging than most run-of-the-mill careers, and the rewards are more satisfying than just money."

With an increasing note of respect in her voice, the clerk completed the form and then personally ushered me to the door.

I had gone on the official records as someone more distinguished and indispensable to mankind than "just another mom."

Although this exchange can be viewed as a humorous anecdote, it is sad to note that there are those in our world who would diminish the role of a mother. The significant impact of mothers on society can never be fully appreciated or articulated. Jael was one of these mothers. She was fulfilling her calling of being a stay-at-home mom and also was in the place God wanted her. It was here, in her tent, where God used this woman to make a tremendous impact on society and on history.

Jael was the wife of Heber the Kenite. We learn that Heber had separated himself from the Kenites and moved near Kedesh. He also had made peace with Jabin, the king of Hazor. (Remember him? He was the enemy.) Their relationship must have been pretty well established because we read that Sisera, after having all of his army and his chariots routed by the Lord, fled away on foot to the tent of Jael.

He went to a place where he thought he could find refuge. Yes, a Jewish household, but one with whom his king had negotiated a peace deal. Besides, Jael was merely a woman in the tent. Sisera could tell her what to do, and she would do it, right? Little did he know that Jael was an informed woman of the tent. She knew the enemy. When he came calling, she recognized him at once.

What about you? Are you able to recognize the enemy when he comes calling?

Our enemy, Satan, is a master of disguise. Second Corinthians 11:14 says he "masquerades as an angel of light." Jael very easily could have seen Sisera as a friend and ally, but astute and alert, she was not tricked. Although Scripture does not elaborate on Jael's thought process, I believe she assessed the situation pretty quickly.

She formulated a plan on the spot. Not only did she invite Sisera in, but she also provided a cover for him and gave him milk when he asked for a drink of water. It didn't take long for that milk to take effect on this exhausted refugee. He soon fell asleep, and that's when Jael knew she could eliminate this enemy once and for all! Jael took a tent peg and a hammer, snuck up on Sisera while he was sleeping, and drove the peg into his temple, killing him immediately!

I realize this is a gruesome story, and to revel in it seems a bit peculiar. But God has given us an amazing perspective through preserving Deborah's song in Judges 5. It is in this song of victory that Jael is honored. Deborah calls it like this:

Most blessed of women is Jael,
> The wife of Heber the Kenite;
> Most blessed is she of women in the tent.

He asked for water and she gave him milk;
> In a magnificent bowl she brought him curds.

She reached out her hand for the tent peg,
> And her right hand for the workmen's hammer.
> Then she struck Sisera, she smashed his head;
> And she shattered and pierced his temple.

Between her feet he bowed, he fell, he lay;
> Between her feet he bowed, he fell;
> Where he bowed, there he fell dead.

Thus let all Your enemies perish, O Lord!
> But let those who love Him be like the rising of the sun
> in its might. (Judges 5:24-27, 31 *NASB*)

God had determined before the battle that the honor of killing Sisera would belong to a woman (Judges 4:9). When we read the story, it seems that Deborah will be the one to have that honor. But Jael, a humble woman in the tent, is the one the song lyrics esteem. Alert and smart, Jael used her calling to bring salvation to her people. The tools of her trade were pitchers and bowls and dairy products! She knew how to wield a hammer because as part of a nomadic family she had the responsibility of putting up and taking down the tent. This woman knew how to use a hammer and a tent peg, and she did it for the glory of God!

Can you understand why Jael is one of my heroes? I think every stay-at-home mom should buy a tent peg and with a black permanent marker write "You Go, Girl!" across it. What an incredible reminder that we can take action and be effective against the enemy, for the glory of God, all while remaining women in the tent.

Day Four: Reflect
Arise

1. Judges 5:9 tells us that Deborah's heart went out to the commanders of Israel. In other words, God stirred up her heart for the cause. We know from the story that she "arose" to fight for that cause.

   List the situations that stir your heart (for example, domestic violence, biblical illiteracy, teenage pregnancies, abortion, cancer, the elderly, etc.).

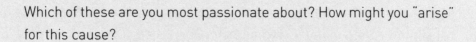

Which of these are you most passionate about? How might you "arise" for this cause?

2. God used both a working woman and a stay-at-home mom for his glory. Daniel 11:32 says, "The people who know their God will display strength and take action" (*NASB*). How did Deborah and Jael each show that they knew God?

Often we may view one calling as higher than another. Based on your studies this week, would you agree or disagree with this idea? Why?

3. Deborah said the honor of the victory over Sisera would belong to a woman. When initially reading the story, we assume that honor will go to Deborah. Deborah might have assumed this as well. In a surprising twist, however, a previously unknown woman named Jael gets the honor for killing the enemy. Deborah's response? She praised and blessed Jael.

How do you typically respond when someone else receives honor and you do not?

What major life lesson can we learn from this?

OBSCURE
Bible Facts

Perhaps Jael had another reason for killing Sisera. "The only male allowed within the curtains of the tent was the husband/father; other men remained in the porch area. Entry of a male stranger within the women's quarters of the tent was punishable by death" (Ralph Gower, *The New Manners and Customs of Bible Times* [Chicago: Moody Press, 1987], 27).

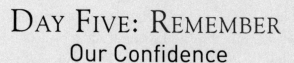

DAY FIVE: REMEMBER
Our Confidence

The story of Deborah and Jael gives us great insights into God's character. I've highlighted a few of them in our closing thoughts for this week.

1. By now you know the drill. Choose a verse to memorize from this week's lesson. Practice saying it over and over. Relay it to friends and family and share with them its significance to you.

2. Continue to add to your list or chart what you learned about God this week.

Knowing God

I've heard it said, "It's not what you know, but who you know that counts." For Deborah and Jael (and for you and me), this adage definitely holds true. Because these two women knew God, they displayed strength and took action in the midst of fearful and abysmal times, and they accomplished great things as a result. But we would be remiss if we attributed the events and the outcome to them. Someone bigger and more powerful worked through them—God himself was orchestrating his plan and his purpose.

Much can be learned about God throughout this story, and knowing our God will enable us to take action as well.

Our Compassionate God

"For the LORD your God is a compassionate God; He will not fail you nor destroy you nor forget the covenant with your fathers which He swore to them" (Deuteronomy 4:31, *NASB*). Despite how far Israel had fallen, God still reached down to help his people out of the hole they had dug. When they cried to him for help, he heard their cries and had compassion on them. God's compassion never ceases to amaze me. Just when we think we have taken the step that will put us out of the embrace of God's arms, he extends his reach to draw us back in.

Have you ever felt you stepped too far? Pushed too hard? Sunk too low? John Wesley, a slave trader, stooped to such sinful lows that even the most vile of men detested his behavior. Yet through a knowledge of God's mercy and grace taught to him as a child, Wesley cried out to God to save him from his sin. And God did. John Wesley wrote the lyrics to the beloved hymn "Amazing Grace."

Our Omniscient God

"See, the former things have taken place, and new things I declare; before they spring into being I announce them to you" (Isaiah 42:9). *Omniscient*. A big word with an even bigger meaning: "having infinite awareness, understanding, and insight."[23] Sometimes I don't believe I have even a *finite* awareness or understanding of anything. Ask my daughter to tell you about the time I forgot to pick her up from preschool—on her first day! Ask my physician husband why I have to be reminded of the dosage of medicine I'm to take every day of my life! Or what about the classes I took in college— could I even begin to explain the science of the citric acid cycle or the mathematical theories behind geometry? That would be a resounding no.

Thankfully, I have a God who can. Not only can he explain them but he created them! He "formed my inward parts" and "wove me in my mother's womb" (Psalm 139:13, *NASB*). I have a God who doesn't forget his child's schedule. He knows when I sit down and when I rise up (Psalms 139:2). He knows and understands my steps and even goes so far as to direct them for me (Proverbs 16:9).

My omniscient, all-knowing, insightful, understanding God is the same God who knew all about Israel's woes during the time of the judges. He knew the Israelites had disobeyed his commands, and he knew they needed to face consequences as a result. God also knew they needed deliverance, and he knew exactly whom he would raise up for that purpose.

Thinking of the infinite knowledge God possesses makes me want to fall down in reverence and awe. How can we doubt him? How can we think we can do things in our own knowledge? Remembering the brilliance and depth of our omniscient Father God will take us far in allowing us to follow his lead.

Our Powerful God

"Who is this King of glory? The LORD strong and mighty, the LORD mighty in battle" (Psalm 24:8). We were stationed in Izmir, Turkey, with the United States Air Force. The day had come for us to move out of our apartment. We lived on the second floor, and all of our appliances had to be carried down to street level. The energetic movers, eager to get started, decided to move the refrigerator first and volunteered the smallest man in their crew to carry it on his back without any assistance! This little guy was shorter than me (I'm only five foot four), and he probably maxed out at 120 pounds soaking wet. His buddies (and I use that term loosely) strapped the refrigerator onto his back and set him in the direction of the staircase. I saw his legs buckle a time or two, but he didn't fall. For what seemed like an eternity but was only a matter of minutes, I watched this little man carry that fridge all the way down to the ground floor without dropping it! He was a sweaty mess, but my refrigerator was intact. Impressive.

I've heard other stories of great strength and have seen such feats on television in competitions to determine the world's strongest man. Mighty and muscular competitors pull trains with merely a shoulder harness. They squat lift large weights, like nine hundred pounds of bricks, a car, or people on a platform. These feats are all impressive to watch, and it's hard to believe that a man can be so strong. Yet these men have only puny strength compared to the might and power possessed by Almighty God!

In the story of Deborah and Sisera, we get a firsthand account of God's strength over a powerful enemy. We learn that "the Lord routed Sisera and all his chariots and army by the sword" (Judges 4:15). We read in Deborah's song that it was the Lord who "marched from the land of Edom" (Judges 5:4). And we hear of his power over nature when Deborah sings, "From the heavens the stars fought, from their courses they fought against Sisera. The river Kishon swept them away" (Judges 5:20, 21).

It was God . . . all God. It was his strength and supremacy over the enemy, the army, and over nature.

Can you feel the power of God? Deborah, Barak, Sisera, and all of Sisera's army not only felt it but also experienced it. God fought the battle for Deborah and Barak. He had everything strapped on his back, so to speak, and he carried it through to completion without dropping it, without legs buckling, without breaking a sweat. That's my God! What confidence we can have knowing the power and might of God! That confidence should spur us on to take action and display strength—the kind that he provides.

Our Surprising God

"For the LORD will rise up as at Mount Perazim, He will be stirred up as in the valley of Gibeon, to do His task, His unusual task, and to work His work, His extraordinary work" (Isaiah 28:21, *NASB*). In his book *God Came Near*, Max Lucado says that God "loves to surprise us out of our socks and be there in the flesh to see our reaction."[24] He must have had a blast as he surprised all of Israel with the upset win over Sisera and his army. The enemy that had oppressed Israel for twenty years was finally taken out. From front-row seats we watch God use surprising things—swords, rain, and mud—to accomplish his goals. Better yet, he surprised ordinary people by using them to do his extraordinary work.

There is hope for us yet, isn't there? With stories of obscure characters of old like Deborah and Jael, we can know that God is waiting and watching for us to do great exploits for him—extraordinary works. He wants to surprise us out of our socks . . . by using *us*! So pull up those knee-highs and get ready, because "the people who know their God will display strength and take action."

What action are you going to take?

OBSCURE OBSERVATIONS

CHAPTER FOUR

Love that reaches up is adoration. Love that reaches across is affection.
Love that reaches down is grace. —Donald Grey Barnhouse

mephibosheth:
an overlooked outcast

KEEPING YOUR WORD • 2 SAMUEL 9

I Called Him Mephibosheth

We were walking through the bazaar in Izmir, Turkey. The shops sold everything from scarves to spices, but the bazaar also provided a form of entertainment for us military family members stationed in a foreign country. And foreign it was. Everything differed from "back home."

The language, of course, was different, but so were the customs and manners. Vendors actively solicited us to come into their shops to buy their wares. They offered hot chai (tea) as well as high compliments, which our ears picked up immediately because they spoke the practiced phrases in our beloved English.

"Pretty lady, would you like some tea?"

"Pretty lady, come here and see my beautiful carpets!"

"I offer you great deal, pretty lady."

Always one for affirmation, I loved going through the various alleys and hearing from shopkeeper to shopkeeper how beautiful I was!

Then I saw him, propped up in a corner.

The entire city of Izmir was laden with hundreds of beggars—glue-sniffing adolescent boys who besieged our car at every stoplight, disillusioned alcoholic men lining the park, weary single moms holding their babies to pull at my heartstrings—the maimed and homeless were everywhere. Considered outcasts by too many, they were the unwelcomed, the invisible, the overlooked. And this man in the bazaar was one of them.

No one paid him any attention. Everyone walked right past him—nearly right over him, a beggar who couldn't hold out a cup. Given the opportunity, he'd probably be like the other beggars and follow after me, but he couldn't walk. He had no arms and no legs.

I tried not to stare, but I couldn't help myself. And as I stood there, he made his way over to me. It was sad . . . pathetic, really, for he used his shoulders and hips to scoot himself along the ground—oh, the dirty, rough, uneven ground! You have to understand: the ground on which he was scooting facedown was covered with filth. A city of nearly four million, Izmir was overcrowded with people, sheep, goats, stray dogs, feral cats, and the garbage they all left behind.

So he scooted toward me. He began speaking in Turkish, which I did not understand. But he effectively communicated when he motioned with his head to the bowl left behind in his corner. It contained a little bit of change, and he made it clear that he wanted me to add to his collection. I did. And then I moved on . . .

Later, I realized that I never asked his name. I wish I had. I'm sure it was something like Ahmet or Ismail or Ozan. But in my mind I called him something else. I called him Mephibosheth.

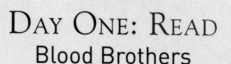

DAY ONE: READ
Blood Brothers

David and Jonathan, best friends. Blood brothers united by a covenant. Even in death their pledge held strong and reached out to an obscure, outcast son named Mephibosheth. So it is with God. This unfamiliar story in 2 Samuel 9 reveals God's unfailing pledge, unrelenting pursuit, and unconditional love. Celebrating our relationship with the ultimate covenant keeper, this lesson invites you to feast at royalty's table and share in the promises paid for by the King of kings himself.

1. Read 1 Samuel 18:1-4. Note the word *covenant* in your Bible. How would you describe the meaning of this word?

•• Word Study •• In order for us to lay a foundation for the rest of this chapter, you will need to do a Hebrew word study on *covenant* (Strong's #1285). Use your Internet resources (remember www.blueletterbible .org) or your own concordance and Hebrew lexicon. Feel free to look at other resources such as Bible encyclopedias to give you more insight on this concept. Be as thorough as you can in your investigation; our week's lesson is built on the foundational principle of covenant.

2. Read 1 Samuel 18:1-4 again and 1 Samuel 20:4-17, 23, 42 about the covenant between King Saul's son Jonathan and David, the shepherd boy who killed Goliath (1 Samuel 17) and eventually became king of Israel in Saul's place.

How far-reaching was this covenant? In other words, how long would it last and whom else would it impact?

What actions were taken in the making of this covenant?

Exchanging robes symbolized an exchange of identities. Kay Arthur, in her book *Our Covenant God*, explains: "By giving David his robe, . . . Jonathan was telling David, 'You're no longer alone—you have a blood brother, a covenant partner. You have put on me!'. . . The exchanging of their robes was . . . an act that said, 'I am so becoming one with you that I will take on your likeness.'"[25]

Of the exchanging of weapons, Arthur says this:

> Remember that covenant was a bond in blood. Therefore, when two people or parties entered into covenant, they understood that everything they had was now held in common, even each other's enemies. Whenever one was under attack, it was the duty of the other to come to his aid.
>
> They were saying, "Because you and I are no longer living independent lives, but are in covenant—and because covenant is the most solemn, binding agreement that can be made between two parties—I am bound by covenant to defend you from your enemies. Those who attack you become my enemies." Thus Jonathan handed David his sword, his bow, and his belt—the belt that held his sword.[26]

Comrades and Covenants

The Bible says that "the soul of Jonathan was knit to the soul of David, and Jonathan loved him as himself" (1 Samuel 18:1, *NASB*). In other words, they were soul mates, the best of friends—Jonathan, the son of King Saul, and David, the shepherd boy turned hero. After David slew the giant Goliath (1 Samuel 17:31-54), Saul quickly made David an integral part of his army. We can assume it was through these events and their mutual relationship with Saul that David and Jonathan became friends. Then they made a *covenant*.

A covenant was serious business, so serious, in fact, that usually an animal was killed in the process to signify the severity of the agreement. Cut in two, the animal was placed on the ground in such a fashion that the blood would drain and flow downward. The parties making the covenant then walked between the pieces of the animal, through the blood—a graphic depiction of the consequences of a broken oath. In other words, those making the agreement were stating, "If I break this oath, may the same thing be done to me as has been done to this animal."

Other symbolic gestures went into the making of a covenant. The exchanging of robes signified the exchange of identities, in essence, becoming one, united. The exchanging of weapons acknowledged the covenant partners' enemies. The agreement bound them to come to each other's aid against their foes.

Sharing a meal was another key element in covenant making. As part of the celebration of the agreement, the meal showed a kind of intimacy and connection between the parties. Several examples of this can be seen in the Old Testament. Covenants between Isaac and Abimelech (Genesis 26:24-30), Laban and Jacob (Genesis 31:44-54), Moses and the elders of Israel (Exodus 24:7-11), and David and Abner (2 Samuel 3:12-20) all incorporated a shared meal.

These binding agreements often included signs of the covenant. One well-known example of a covenant sign is *circumcision*, the sign instituted by God in his covenant with Abraham. Another well-known example of a covenant sign, the rainbow, appeared to Noah and his family: "This is the sign of the covenant I am making between me and you and every living creature with you, a covenant for all generations to come: I have set my rainbow in the clouds, and it will be the sign of the covenant between me and the earth. . . . Whenever the rainbow appears in the clouds, I will see it and remember the everlasting covenant between God and all living creatures of every kind on the earth" (Genesis 9:12, 13, 16).

Finally, covenants could extend from generation to generation. Not only did the covenant we just read about between God and Noah depict this, but Jonathan and David included these terms in their agreement with each other as well. Jonathan said, "Go in peace, for we have sworn friendship with each other in the name of the LORD, saying, 'The LORD is witness between you and me, and between your descendants and my descendants forever'" (1 Samuel 20:42).

Serious. Binding. Intimate. Long lasting. Sealed with a sign. Covenants were not to be entered into lightly.

········•◦●◦•········

Day Two: Read
For Jonathan's Sake

1. Read 2 Samuel 4:4; 9.

2. List all the facts you learn about Mephibosheth.

Read 1 Samuel 31:4-7. What was the report that caused Mephibosheth's nurse to flee in such a hurry?

After Saul's death God established David as king of Israel (2 Samuel 5:3, 12). Oftentimes, incoming kings assassinated any and all of the previous king's remaining family members to ensure the security of their new throne. Knowing this background, why do you think Mephibosheth's nurse left in such haste?

3. What did David request?

Why was he looking for Saul's family members?

David learned of a son of Jonathan who was still alive. What did he do in response?

From the text, how much time do you think had elapsed between Mephibosheth's being injured as a boy and being summoned by David?

4. What was Mephibosheth's emotional response to the summons? Why did he react that way? How did he view himself?

What did David offer Mephibosheth?

How often did Mephibosheth eat at David's table? Who was Mephibosheth likened to?

5. Think back over all you have learned the past two days. Why do you think David acted as he did toward Mephibosheth?

········•●●●•········

DAY THREE: RELATE
Promises, Promises

The story of David and Jonathan's covenant and the fulfillment of the covenant promises to Mephibosheth give us a beautiful picture of God's relationship with us. Many scholars believe the principle of covenant is the foundation on which God operates. It would behoove us then to make sure we know a little about it, right?

Because understanding this concept is crucial to understanding God's redemptive work, we need to spend more time looking at certain aspects of covenant. The main covenant we will focus on is the one God made with Abraham (called Abram at this point), recorded in Genesis 15. Blood of innocent animals was shed to solidify and show in picture form the seriousness of the agreement. The covenant included several promises, and those promises are reiterated throughout Genesis. Let's look at Genesis 17 to get the full view of the promises associated with this Abrahamic covenant:

. . . .

When Abram was ninety-nine years old, the LORD appeared to him and said, "I am God Almighty; walk before me and be blameless. I will confirm my covenant between me and you and will greatly increase your numbers."

Abram fell facedown, and God said to him, "As for me, this is my covenant with you: You will be the father of many nations. No longer will you be called Abram; your name will be Abraham, for I have made you a father of many nations. I will make you very fruitful; I will make nations of you, and kings will come from you. I will establish my covenant as an everlasting covenant between me and you and your descendants after you for the generations to come, to be your God and the God of your descendants after you. The whole land of Canaan, where you are now an alien, I will give as an everlasting possession to you and your descendants after you; and I will be their God." (Genesis 17:1-8)

. . . .

1. Highlight the clause "I will" throughout the passage. Then list all that God promised to do.

2. How long will this covenant last?

With whom is this covenant in effect?

Cross-reference Abraham's descendants by looking up Galatians 3:7-9. Does this impact your answer to the previous question?

What does this mean for you?

3. Making a covenant included several aspects:

- The shedding of blood (Genesis 15:9, 10)

- The exchanging of robes and weapons (1 Samuel 18:1-4)

- A sign—in this case the sign was circumcision (Genesis 17:11)

- Making promises (Genesis 17:1-8)

- Eating a meal together (Genesis 26:26-30)

Mephibosheth received an invitation to regularly share his meals with King David. We too feast at our King's table regularly. Read 1 Corinthians 11:23-26. Explain how this passage relates to a covenant meal. Do you see any other aspects of covenant in this passage?

Does our feasting with our King end when we leave this earth? Read Revelation 19:9 and write down what you learn.

DAY FOUR: REFLECT
I See "Me" in Mephibosheth

1. What was Mephibosheth's position and status before he met King David?

What was his position and status after he met the king?

Compare yourself to Mephibosheth. Can you relate to him in any sense? If so, how?

2. What city was Mephibosheth residing in?

●● Word Study ●● Do a word study on the Hebrew place name Lo Debar (Lo-debar, Strong's #3810 and #1699). What does the name of that city mean?

Your word study should have revealed the name to mean "not a pasture" or "without a fold." *Lo* means "without" and *deber* means "pasture, fold, manner."[27] Knowing the Hebrew definition, can you describe Mephibosheth's spiritual condition without his father's covenant with David?

What would our spiritual condition be without our King's covenant with us?

3. Consider what we have because of that covenant:

. . . .

Praise be to the God and Father of our Lord Jesus Christ, who has blessed us in the heavenly realms with every spiritual blessing in Christ. For he chose us in him before the creation of the world to be holy and blameless in his sight. In love he predestined us to be adopted as his sons through Jesus Christ, in accordance with his pleasure and will—to the praise of his glorious grace, which he has freely given us in the one he loves. In him we have redemption through his blood, the forgiveness of sins, in accordance with the riches of God's grace that he lavished on us with all wisdom and understanding. And he made known to us the mystery of his will according to his good pleasure, which he purposed in Christ, to be put into effect when the times will have reached their fulfillment—to bring all things in heaven and on earth together under one head, even Christ.

In him we were also chosen, having been predestined according to the plan of him who works out everything in conformity with the purpose of his will, in order that we, who were the first to hope in Christ, might be for the praise of his glory. And you also were included in Christ when you heard the word of truth, the gospel of your salvation. Having believed, you were marked in him with a seal, the promised Holy Spirit, who is a deposit guaranteeing our inheritance until the redemption of those who are God's possession—to the praise of his glory. (Ephesians 1:3-14)

Highlight the phrase "in him" and "in Christ" throughout the passage. Then list all that we have in Jesus.

Knowing this, how should we view ourselves? How should we view other "Mephibosheths"?

Connections

So what do two comrades and a covenant have to do with a man named Mephibosheth? Let me explain.

King Saul and three of his sons, including Jonathan, all died on the same day during the same battle. Two years later, Saul's fourth son was murdered by two of Saul's commanders, effectively ending the dynasty. Word got back to the royal family, and they were royally scared! They fled for their lives, and in the rush the little five-year-old son of Jonathan fell and was crippled for life. This crippled boy, Mephibosheth, ended up in hiding in a place called Lo Debar.

In the meantime, David became king of Israel. He ruled for several years and had great success as king. Then one day he asked, "Is there anyone still left of the house of Saul to whom I can show kindness for Jonathan's sake?" (2 Samuel 9:1). A servant who had served under Saul spoke up: "There is still a son of Jonathan; he is crippled in both feet" (v. 3). King David sent for this crippled son, and when Mephibosheth came before the king, he bowed and said, "What is your servant, that you should notice a dead dog like me?" (v. 8).

A dead dog? What was Mephibosheth talking about?

A dead dog was how Mephibosheth viewed himself! Think about it. A dead dog had no value, no worth. In Jewish culture dogs were considered digusting scavengers. And here was Mephibosheth, living in the home of Machir (not even a relative) in a town called Lo Debar, which in Hebrew means "without a pasture" or "outside the fold." In other words, Mephibosheth didn't belong. He had no place and no one who claimed him. No one who loved him. No one who accepted him. Now all of a sudden, the *king* had called him? With great trepidation Mephibosheth came before David. Maybe he expected to be put to death. Maybe his proclaiming himself a dead dog was a prophesy in his fear-filled mind!

But David completely surprised him and said, "I will surely show you kindness for the sake of your father Jonathan" (v. 7). In other words, "Guess what, Mephibosheth? I made a covenant with your dad—and that covenant extends to you! Your inheritance will be restored, and you can eat at my table . . . regularly! And it gets even better . . . because you're going to be like one of my sons."

I'm sure Mephibosheth by now was thinking, *Way to go, Dad! Great foresight including that extension clause, because now I'm covered!*

You're probably beginning to feel as if you're part of an infomercial—"But wait! That's not all!" And rightly so, because that's *not* all. "Mephibosheth had a young son named Mica" (v. 12). The extension clause not only took care of Mephibosheth but his young son too. Imagine how much that must have meant to a man lame in both feet. His son would be provided for!

The last verse of 2 Samuel 9 gives us a great summary: "And Mephibosheth lived in Jerusalem, because he always ate at the king's table, and he was crippled in both feet" (v. 13). It's kind of like a before-and-after shot of Mephibosheth's life. Before, he lived in Lo Debar, a place for those who didn't belong. Now he lived in Jerusalem, the city of the king. Before, he lived secretly in the seclusion of a stranger's home. Now he ate openly at the king's table like one of the king's sons.

Think about the before part of Mephibosheth's life. Maybe we're not so different from this crippled outcast. Maybe some of his problems hit a little closer to home than we care to admit:

- Here's a guy—alive for years who never really lived. Unfulfilled. (Have you ever experienced that?)

- Here's a man—a virtual prisoner in a stranger's house. Not free. (What prison is holding you?)

- Here's someone—hiding year after year. Fearful. (Fear itself can be crippling, you know.)

● Hanging out in Lo Debar—a place outside the fold. He didn't belong. Guided? Cared for? Fed and protected? People who mattered received that kind of attention. Not him. (Can you relate?)

But a covenant between two comrades made all the difference in the world for Mephibosheth. And another covenant, made thousands of years ago, can make all the difference in our world too.

DAY FIVE: REMEMBER
An Attitude of Gratitude

1. Memorize your favorite verse from this week's lesson. Why is it your favorite?

2. What things have you learned about God this week? Add those things to your list or chart.

3. My husband and I have tried to instill in our children an attitude of appreciation. One way we have done this is by requiring them to write thank-you notes when they receive gifts of any kind from friends and family. Spend some time right now writing a thank-you note to Jesus. It may seem simplistic, and I realize our words might be inadequate, but I feel pretty confident that God would love to hear what you have to say!

Covenant Cares

God made an everlasting covenant thousands of years ago with a man named Abraham; a covenant that would extend and continues to extend to Abraham's descendants. And who are Abraham's descendants? Galatians 3:7 defines them as those who have faith in Jesus Christ.

This covenant was made like the ones mentioned earlier—animals cut in two . . . blood trickling, flowing between the pieces—but for this covenant God said, "I'm the one who's going to walk between the pieces. I'm the one who is going to be responsible for *both* ends of the deal. I know I'm not going to break it. But if you break the contract, I will pay the price for you."

And guess what? We broke the contract. We broke it when we sinned, and we all have sinned (Romans 3:23). That sin forced us to live "outside the fold," considered as dead dogs.

"But God" (don't you love that phrase?) "demonstrates his own love for us in this: While we were still sinners, Christ died for us" (Romans 5:8).

He paid the price the contract required.

That dead dog, me—I was made alive again.

And that dead dog, you—you have been restored!

You and I have been offered an invitation . . . by *the* King!

We can feast at his table regularly.

We're considered his sons and daughters.

We've been given an inheritance.

And we've been granted a life that is fulfilling . . .

and free . . .

and fearless.

Oh, and did I mention I was lame in both feet?

Yes. I once was lame in both feet . . . but now I've been made to walk!

I once was in prison . . . but now I've been set free!

I once was blind . . . but now I see!

Amazing, isn't it?

Are you amazed? Then be restored.

Are you amazed? Then accept his invitation. Come to the table.

Because this is amazing, you know.

It's amazing . . . grace.

OBSCURE
Bible Facts

Having a crippled foot is just one of the physical defects listed in Leviticus 21 that would prevent a descendant of Aaron from entering the sanctuary of God. "The LORD said to Moses, "Say to Aaron: 'For the generations to come none of your descendants who has a defect may come near to offer the food of his God. No man who has any defect may come near: no man who is blind or lame, disfigured or deformed; no man with a crippled foot or hand, or who is hunchbacked or dwarfed, or who has any eye defect, or who has festering or running sores or damaged testicles. . . . He may eat the most holy food of his God, as well as the holy food; yet because of his defect, he must not go near the curtain or approach the altar, and so desecrate my sanctuary. I am the LORD, who makes them holy'" (Leviticus 21:16-23).

But Jesus healed people who were crippled and also gave them a place at the table (see Luke 14:12-14).

OBSCURE OBSERVATIONS

CHAPTER FIVE

"I'm the king of the world!"
—Leonardo DiCaprio as Jack Dawson in *Titanic*

adonijah:
a wannabe king

SURRENDERING CONTROL • 1 KINGS 1

Lights, Camera, Action!

People can be obsessed with movies, spending billions each year on tickets, DVDs, and downloads. Conversations over coffee and around the watercooler often involve movie characters, plots, and personal critiques. Even our news channels report box-office standings. Famous phrases such as "I'll get you, my pretty, and your little dog, too!"[28] or "I am your father" conjure up story lines with good guys, bad guys, conflicts, and climaxes. Yes, we are fans of the movies—fascinated by the performances, fixated on the drama. But let me tell you, Hollywood has nothing on the Bible!

Sixty-six smaller books in one, the Bible contains countless stories Hollywood might wish to mine. Intricately woven plots, multifaceted characters, depth, intrigue, comedy, tragedy, climactic eleventh-hour resolutions—the Bible has it all, *and* it is all real—true, accurate, inspiring, dramatic.

And if awards were given out for Best Bible Drama, the story we will study this week would definitely be in the running. So dim the lights, butter the popcorn, and get ready to immerse yourself in a real-life drama found in the pages of Scripture.

DAY ONE: READ
Best Actor in a Leading Role

In order to understand the drama, let's spend time reading the chapter and figuring out the cast of characters—including the leading man.

1. Read through 1 Kings 1.

2. Read through the chapter a second time. This time, using two differently colored pencils, highlight the names Adonijah and Solomon and all the pronouns referring to them.

3. The chapter can be divided up into scenes. In the list that follows, read the verses and write a title for the scene.

Scene	Title
vv. 1-10	
vv. 11-14	
vv. 15-21	
vv. 22-27	
vv. 28-31	
vv. 32-37	

Scene	Title
vv. 38-40	
vv. 41-48	
vv. 49-53	

The Backstory

"A long time ago, in a galaxy far, far away . . ." —*Star Wars*

As with any good drama, you've got to know a bit of the backstory to have a full appreciation of events as they unfold. A backstory is the story behind the story, so to speak. And before our main character Adonijah makes his appearance, we need to review some history.

As we open the pages of the book of 1 Kings, the first thing we read is this: "When King David was old and well advanced in years, he could not keep warm even when they put covers over him" (1 Kings 1:1). In other words, King David was dying.

Remember David, who slew the giant Goliath? All Israel hailed him a hero (1 Samuel 17). The shepherd boy in whom God saw great potential (1 Samuel 16:1-13), the one God said was a man after his own heart (1 Samuel 13:14), became the great King David, who served God's purpose for his generation (Acts 13:36). Now the highly revered patriarch was dying, and the kingdom would soon need a new king.

In keeping with the twists and turns we so love in a good drama, David's servants did what they thought was best for their old, cold king: "So his servants said to him, 'Let us look for a young virgin to attend the king and take care of him. She can lie beside him so that our lord the king may keep warm.' Then they searched throughout Israel for a beautiful girl and found Abishag, a Shunammite, and brought her to the king" (1 Kings 1:2, 3).

Evidently these servants thought Abishag would help the old man's temperature. After all, a little extra body heat could go a long way in keeping the king comfortable. However, the night did not get steamy; as we read in the next verse, David "had no intimate relations with her" (v. 4). Perhaps the king had gotten cold in his old age, but he seemed to have gained some wisdom too (2 Samuel 11, 12; Psalm 51). Maybe there is something to be said about learning from past mistakes! He'd have to remember to thank Nathan and Bathsheba the next time he saw them. Anyway . . .

Let's reiterate what we know. The old, cold king was dying. The kingdom would soon need a new king. God himself had made a covenant with David—David's throne would be established forever (1 Chronicles 22:10). Typically a throne is handed down to the oldest living son. This would have assured Adonijah the kingship, for he was David's oldest living son at that time. But God had a different plan, and birth order had nothing to do with it. David understood this message from the Lord and had shared it with Israel: "Of all my sons—and the LORD has given me many—he has chosen my son Solomon to sit on the throne of the kingdom of the LORD over Israel" (1 Chronicles 28:5).

Do you feel the tension in the room? Do you sense that things are about to break loose? Hold on to your seat, because the drama is just beginning to play out!

DAY TWO: READ
Best Original Screenplay

1. The cast of characters in this story can be a little overwhelming. To better understand the players, make a list of those who supported Adonijah and those who supported Solomon.

Adonijah   Solomon

2. Each of these characters also had a relationship of some sort with David. Before we delve into their backstories, let's identify David and the situation in which he found himself. Who was David?

At what stage of life was he?

How prominent does his role as king seem to have been at this point? Why do you say that?

3. First Kings 1 names all those in the list that follows. Describe the relationship of each of these people with David. Use the Scripture references for additional information if you need it.

Abishag

Adonijah (2 Samuel 3:2-4)

Joab (2 Samuel 8:16)

Abiathar (1 Samuel 22:20-23; 2 Samuel 20:25)

Zadok (2 Samuel 20:25)

Benaiah (2 Samuel 8:18)

Nathan (2 Samuel 12)

Solomon (2 Samuel 12:24)

Bathsheba (2 Samuel 11:3-5; 12:24)

4. What do you learn from 1 Kings 1 about David's relationship with Adonijah? How did the two men interact?

How is Adonijah described? (vv. 5, 6)

Why is that information in the text? What insight into Adonijah's character does it give?

5. This story line involves many players, but let's not overlook the director—the one who was (and is) in control of everything. According to 1 Kings 1:17, what did God promise about his intentions for Solomon?

Read 1 Chronicles 22:6-10, 17-19. Who knew that Solomon was to be the next king?

Why did David say Solomon would be the next king?

Read 1 Chronicles 28:1-8. Who knew that Solomon was to be the next king? (I know this sounds redundant, but . . .)

From these passages why did David say Solomon would be the next king?

The Plot Thickens

"Houston, we have a problem." —Tom Hanks as Jim Lovell in *Apollo 13*

The camera pans the room and focuses on the door. Sinister theme music plays in the background, rising to a rapid climax as the door opens with great force. Adonijah enters the room. "Now Adonijah the son of Haggith exalted himself, saying, 'I will be king.' So he prepared for himself chariots and horsemen with fifty men to run before him. . . . He had conferred with Joab the son of Zeruiah and with Abiathar the priest; and following Adonijah they helped him" (1 Kings 1:5, 7, *NASB*).

The Conflict

"Go ahead, make my day." —Clint Eastwood as Harry Callahan in *Sudden Impact*

I don't know what kind of theme music you are imagining, but the music in my mind is from the movie *Jaws*. Here is a big fish, so to speak, readying himself for an attack! As I mentioned earlier, at this point Adonijah was David's oldest living son. We also learn from the Bible that he was a "very handsome man" and "his father never crossed him at any time" (v. 6, *NASB*). I'd be willing to bet Adonijah was used to getting what he wanted, when he wanted it. And now he wanted the kingdom.

He rallied big support: Joab, the commander of David's army, and Abiathar, David's priest. Serious about his plans to take over the kingdom, Adonijah went at it with serious allies. He also went about it with great pomp and circumstance. Not only did he set up his own parade to trumpet his kingship; he also threw a coronation party and invited a chosen group to celebrate his rise to the throne: "Adonijah then sacrificed sheep, cattle and fattened calves at the Stone of Zoheleth near En Rogel. He invited all his brothers, the king's sons, and all the men of [the tribe of] Judah who were royal officials, but he did not invite Nathan the prophet or Benaiah or the special guard or his brother Solomon" (1 Kings 1:9, 10).

Adonijah seemed to have it all figured out. He knew whom he wanted in his camp and whom he did not. But he neglected to realize that no number of men, commanders, or priests could change the outcome of the supreme and absolute will of our sovereign, almighty God!

The Confrontation
"Hasta la vista, baby." —Arnold Schwarzenegger in *Terminator 2: Judgment Day*

We are not told the details, but somehow Nathan the *prophet* (a spokesman for God), one of those on the do-not-invite list, heard of Adonijah's plot. Nathan was the one, if you recall, who knew of David and Bathsheba's affair and was given the undesirable task of confronting the king with his sin (2 Samuel 12). Once again, Nathan's role was to inform the king of unpleasantries. This time, however, he had Bathsheba on his side. Nathan met with Bathsheba, now one of David's wives and the mother of Solomon, and convinced her to go before the king to inform him of the situation with

Adonijah. Nathan recommended that Bathsheba remind the king of his promise that Solomon would sit on the throne. Nathan planned to come in while this conversation took place and would confirm Bathsheba's words.

Bathsheba followed Nathan's counsel and talked with the king. Nathan came running into the room and confirmed what she said. Well, the old, cold king suddenly got a little hot under the collar and decided to take matters into his own hands:

. . . .

King David said, "Call in Zadok the priest, Nathan the prophet and Benaiah son of Jehoiada." When they came before the king, he said to them: "Take your lord's servants with you and set Solomon my son on my own mule and take him down to Gihon. There have Zadok the priest and Nathan the prophet anoint him king over Israel. Blow the trumpet and shout, 'Long live King Solomon!' Then you are to go up with him, and he is to come and sit on my throne and reign in my place. I have appointed him ruler over Israel and Judah." (1 Kings 1:32-35)

. . . .

The outcome? Solomon became king. The people rejoiced, so exuberantly in fact that "the ground shook with the sound" (v. 40). And get this: the noise was so great that the guests at Adonijah's coronation party heard it. When they began wondering about the racket, a messenger came in and told everyone King David had blessed Solomon and made him king! Their reaction? They "rose in alarm and dispersed" (v. 49). So much for supporting "king" Adonijah. At this point, it was every man for himself!

True to form, Adonijah made his exit a dramatic one. Upon hearing that Solomon had been crowned, Adonijah attempted to find sanctuary at the altar, hanging onto its horns like a child calling safe on base in a game of hide-and-seek! Not only that but he had the gall to use Bathsheba as his messenger to bring a marriage request before Solomon. Adonijah wanted Abishag (the warm body brought in for King David) to be his wife! Solomon understood that this request was a last-ditch effort to undermine his kingship, and Adonijah's actions led to his inevitable execution.

The drama is over the top, wouldn't you say? Yet through it all there is truly only one who deserves the attention. You see, while the story line unfolded, our sovereign God knew the final act from the beginning and saw to it that Solomon was firmly established on the throne of David. This divine director, Jehovah God (Exodus 6:3), thus fulfilled his promise to David, the man after God's own heart (1 Samuel 13:14).

OBSCURE
Bible Facts

"The 'horns of the altar' were of one piece with the frame of the altar of burnt offering. . . . A person seeking sanctuary might catch hold of the horns of the altar in the temple, but this did not save Adonijah" (Merrill C. Tenney, *The Zondervan Pictorial Bible Dictionary* [Grand Rapids: Zondervan Publishing House, 1967], 361).

DAY THREE: RELATE
Best Director

A lot of manipulating goes on in this story! Everyone seemed to claim a right to something and did all he could to make sure his rights and plans came to fruition. But who really directed it all?

1. Read 1 Kings 2:12-15, 45, 46 and write a synopsis of what you learn.

2. Does God truly work like this—establishing kings and kingdoms? Read the following passages of Scripture and then work through the instructions after each one:

And [Daniel] said:

"Praise be to the name of God for ever and ever;
wisdom and power are his.

He changes times and seasons;
he sets up kings and deposes them.
He gives wisdom to the wise
and knowledge to the discerning.

He reveals deep and hidden things;
he knows what lies in darkness,
and light dwells with him.

I thank and praise you, O God of my fathers:
You have given me wisdom and power,
you have made known to me what we asked of you,
you have made known to us the dream of the king."
(Daniel 2:20-23)

Highlight every reference to God.

Underline the things God does.

Circle the things God gives.

Remember the former things, those of long ago;
  I am God, and there is no other;
  I am God, and there is none like me.

I make known from the beginning,
  from ancient times, what is still to come.
  I say: My purpose will stand,
  and I will do all that I please.

From the east I summon a bird of prey;
  from a far-off land, a man to fulfill my purpose.
  What I have said, that will I bring about;
  what I have planned, that will I do. (Isaiah 46:9-11)

Highlight every reference to God.

Underline the things God does.

Where can I go from your Spirit?
  Where can I flee from your presence?

If I go up to the heavens, you are there;
  if I make my bed in the depths, you are there.

If I rise on the wings of the dawn,
  if I settle on the far side of the sea,

even there your hand will guide me,
  your right hand will hold me fast.

If I say, "Surely the darkness will hide me
          and the light become night around me,"

even the darkness will not be dark to you;
          the night will shine like the day,
                    for darkness is as light to you. (Psalm 139:7-12)

Highlight every reference to God.

Draw a box around every place God is.

Underline what God does.

DAY FOUR: REFLECT
Best Adapted Screenplay

This week I've directed your thoughts toward a specific lesson to be learned from Adonijah, that God is sovereign—having supreme authority and power. There is always so much more to a passage of Scripture or a Bible character's story than just the one lesson, however. So today, rather than honing in on what I want you to see, let's allow you the opportunity to glean your own life lessons.

1. Read through 1 Kings 1 again. This time ask God to open your eyes to see what he would have *you* learn through the story of Adonijah. You might notice lessons about any of the following areas. Don't feel that you must relate to each topic. Rather, use the list as a guide or catalyst for discovering truths that may be pertinent to your own life.

Parenting

Relationships

God's plans vs. man's plans

Wisdom

Forgiveness

Keeping your word

Holding grudges

Confronting sin

Betrayal

Manipulating circumstances

_____ (Fill in the blank!)

2. Which lesson do you connect with most? Circle it. Now, using any Bible study tools you have, dig a little deeper to see what else you can learn about that topic. Find other passages that will broaden or support the lesson. Write out a synopsis of your lesson and how it applies to your life.

Life Lessons from a Drama King

"Carpe diem. Seize the day, boys. Make your lives extraordinary." —Robin Williams as John Keating in *Dead Poets Society*

Adonijah—intriguing story, isn't it? And straight from the pages of Scripture! No scriptwriter had to be hired to make up this drama. More than just intriguing and interesting, though, are the relevant life lessons we can take away from this saga.

Our Rights Are Not Always Right

"Nobody puts Baby in a corner." —Patrick Swayze as Johnny Castle in *Dirty Dancing*

People like to talk about their rights. The first ten amendments to the U.S. Constitution (the Bill of Rights) include the right to exercise freedom of religion, speech, and the press; the right to peaceably assemble; the right to keep and bear arms; and the right not to undergo unreasonable searches and seizures. All citizens of the United States are guaranteed these rights. Upon further research, though, I found that many people believe their rights go way beyond those found in the Constitution.

There are those who believe in their right to be happy. Some express their right to be rude. I've read about smokers' rights, patients' rights, taxicab riders' rights . . . even pornographers' rights! There are petitions for the right to be lazy, the right to lie, the right to dream, to rock, and to romance. Years ago the Beastie Boys sang a song with this line: "You gotta fight for your right to party."[29] I think I can say that we all believe we have a right to something!

But are these real rights or only perceived? Are they *right* rights or are they wrong?

Societal norms and conventional wisdom tell us to lay hold of our rights. But is conventional wisdom the truth? Is conventional wisdom of God or does it follow the world? Is there a difference? The book of James highlights two very different kinds of wisdom:

Who is wise and understanding among you? Let him show it by his good life, by deeds done in the humility that comes from wisdom. But if you harbor bitter envy and selfish ambition in your hearts, do not boast about it or deny the truth. Such "wisdom" does not come down from heaven but is earthly, unspiritual, of the devil. For where you have envy and selfish ambition, there you find disorder and every evil practice.

> But the wisdom that comes from heaven is first of all pure; then peace-loving, considerate, submissive, full of mercy and good fruit, impartial and sincere. Peacemakers who sow in peace raise a harvest of righteousness. (James 3:13-18)

. . . .

We see two kinds of wisdom in this passage: earthly wisdom and wisdom from heaven. The kind of wisdom Adonijah had in seeking the kingship was earthly. His actions exemplified selfish ambition and arrogance. He went against the truth spoken not only by his father, David, but also by God. As a result there was "disorder and every evil practice" (James 3:16).

We know that Adonijah lost his life, but if you read on in Kings you'll find that those who supported him suffered their own demise as well. Adonijah's actions reaped a harvest of dire consequences. His "rights" were wrong because they went against God's plan. Had Adonijah sought wisdom from above, his life and many others' lives might have served a higher purpose. His life's harvest would have yielded good fruit.

What about you? Do you seek wisdom from above, or do you follow the wisdom of this earth? Is there something you feel you deserve or have a right to? Have you asked God and sought his wisdom regarding your situation?

Beware the Company You Keep!

"Mama says, 'Stupid is as stupid does.'" —Michael Conner Humphreys as young Forrest Gump in *Forrest Gump*

My mom and dad used to tell me, "You can discern a man's character by the company he keeps." Over the years I have learned there is much truth in this statement. Joab and Abiathar, two of the men who supported Adonijah, would have done well to heed such advice. Although we aren't told specifically why each of these men decided to join Adonijah's bid for the throne, we can assume they had selfish ambitions, for they were already in the service of a king: Joab was David's long-time military commander and Abiathar was David's priest.

Solomon penned these interesting words: "My son, if sinners entice you, do not give in to them. If they say, . . . 'Throw in your lot with us, and we will share a common purse'—my son, do not go along with them, do not set foot on their paths; for their feet rush into sin, they are swift to shed blood" (Proverbs 1:10, 11, 14-16). Solomon's experience with Adonijah, Joab, and Abiathar must have had some influence on the wisdom he expresses here. If Joab and Abiathar could have regarded such wisdom, they might have been spared their unfortunate ends. Joab was executed; Abiathar lost the priesthood. Their association with Adonijah revealed their character and sealed their fate. Solomon himself handed down their sentences (1 Kings 2).

With whom have you joined yourself? Although Christ followers are called to be salt and light in this world (Matthew 5:13, 14), the Bible makes it very clear that we are not to be friends with the world. In fact, James says, "Anyone who chooses to be a friend of the world becomes an enemy of God" (James 4:4). This friendship of which he speaks is a deep, committed relationship, with a sense of partnership or joining together. Remember our discussion of covenants in chapter 4? A covenant binds two parties together as one. James is saying that if you are a friend of the world, you have joined yourself with the ways of the world. This friendship, then, would make you an enemy of God.

Joab and Abiathar formed a partnership with a man who blatantly defied God's plan. They were not careful in their association, and they ended up reaping the consequences. What about you? Do you need to take inventory of your close relationships? Are they helping you draw nearer to God or are they pulling you farther and farther away? Pay attention to the lesson from Joab and Abiathar: Beware the company you keep!

God Is Sovereign

"Of all the gin joints in all the towns in all the world, she walks into mine."
—Humphrey Bogart as Rick Blaine in *Casablanca*

Just recently my son and daughter auditioned for parts in the play *Narnia.* Over eighty kids tried out for the various roles. The small number of parts in comparison with the number of children trying out made casting the characters a difficult task for the director. I found it interesting to watch and listen to those in the audience make judgments about who would be best for each of the roles. They thought they knew with certainty how the casting would pan out. But when the cast list was posted several days later, some of the choices caused great shock.

The decisions, explained the director, would stand. Although she and members of the casting committee had debated greatly over the various roles, as the director she had the final say.

The role of the successor to David's throne was *not* to be Adonijah's, even though Adonijah thought it should be. He wanted it; therefore, he would have it—in his world that's how things worked. He had lived by that inverted, self-absorbed thinking for years! But the ultimate director had already determined the cast of characters in this story. From times past God had set forth his plan for the nation of Israel. Adonijah neglected to realize that the play had already been written, the characters had already been cast. Although he felt he knew the right people for the parts, his was not the final word. That word belonged to the Lord God, Jehovah, God Almighty. He is immeasurably bigger than our finite minds can begin to fathom, yet he is intimately involved in the affairs of men.

Adonijah, thinking he could thwart God's plan, showed he had a bit of a God complex. Actually, we are not so different from Adonijah. (Kind of scary, isn't it?) If you are honest, I'm sure you can think of *at least one* situation where you tried to do things your own way. You thought you could handle everything on your own. You thought you knew best.

We tend to forget we are not in control. God has a plan and a purpose. That he allows you and me to participate should amaze us! Do we honestly believe we know better than God? What fools we are! No matter what Adonijah did, it was not going to stop God's already established design for Israel. Adonijah would not be king. Over and over we read in 1 Kings 2 that Solomon's kingdom was established, and there is no mistaking who did the establishing!

What about in your life? Are you trying to manipulate circumstances or people to accommodate your plans? If so, remember this lesson from a drama king: God is sovereign. He is the one who writes the script. Trust him to know what is best for your story.

DAY FIVE: REMEMBER
And the Oscar Goes To . . .

1. Memorize a verse from this week's lesson. You choose. Write it out and say it out loud at least three times.

2. What did you learn about God this week? Add it to your list or chart.

A Lesson from Melman

"I feel the need . . . the need for speed!" —Tom Cruise and Anthony Edwards as Lts. Pete "Maverick" Mitchell and Nick "Goose" Bradshaw in *Top Gun*

I remember a time when I wanted a new car. I didn't *need* a new car. The "old" one ran fine; we even had it paid off. Just tired of it, I wanted a new car, and I wanted it now! (Sounds a bit Adonijah-esque, doesn't it?)

One Friday evening when our kids spent the night with their grandparents, I suggested to my husband that we go to a local car dealership's Midnight Madness sale. (*Big* mistake . . . you should never even *think* of making a major purchase during the sleeping hours of normal people!) Against my husband's better judgment, he drove me to the dealership.

More than once he said we needed to pray about this decision and tried to persuade me to leave. But I was determined. My need for—no, my *right to*—a new car overruled any sense of spirituality. God would be fine with us buying a new vehicle—I felt certain.

So by 1 AM we drove home in our new SUV! What a thrill! This couldn't be a selfish thing at all! I needed it! I deserved it! It was my right! Right?

Wrong. Three transmissions and one depleted savings account later, we no longer own Melman. (My kids affectionately named our car Melman after a hypochondriac cartoon giraffe.) Lesson learned. I should have sought God's wisdom and not my own.

Our perceived rights tempt us to take action. Our actions bring about consequences. So why not seek God's wisdom *before* acting? We are not fated to watch everything fall apart. We can be witnesses to the peaceable, reasonable, unwavering ways of God . . . recipients of his blessings instead! So think about this: the next time you want to exercise your "rights," ask God what he wants you to do. James 1:5 says, "If any of you lacks wisdom, let him ask of God, who gives to all generously and without reproach, and it will be given to him" (*NASB)*.

Ask. He'll dole out wisdom generously. Now that's *right*.

OBSCURE OBSERVATIONS

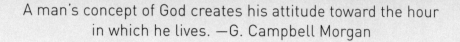

CHAPTER SIX

A man's concept of God creates his attitude toward the hour
in which he lives. —G. Campbell Morgan

jehoshaphat:
a God-seeking leader

LETTING GO OF FEAR • 2 CHRONICLES 20

More Than a Song

For years one of the only things I knew about Jehoshaphat was that his name could be sung to the tune of the end of the Mickey Mouse Club theme song. *Jehoshaphat* has exactly the same number of letters as *Mickey Mouse*. Try it (you remember the tune, don't you?): J-E-H . . . O-S-H . . . A-P-H-A-T.

I acquired this great knowledge as a middle schooler at church camp. We kids were placed into teams, each team had to be named after one of the kings in the Bible, and . . . we needed a team song. M-I-C . . . K-E-Y . . .

Unfortunately, that was the extent of my education regarding King Jehoshaphat. Looking back, I wish my team leader had shown me more and taken me deeper into the story of Jehoshaphat, because he lived a life full of lessons pertinent not only to middle-schoolers but to middle-agers—and everyone in between and beyond.

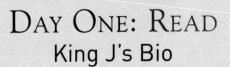

DAY ONE: READ
King J's Bio

Our goal for today is to glean a little bit of information about Jehoshaphat's character and put together a short bio about him.

1. Jehoshaphat was one of the eight good kings of Judah. We can learn the reasons by looking at the following verses:

   2 Chronicles 17:3-6. List the reasons why the Lord was with Jehoshaphat.

   2 Chronicles 17:7-9. What purpose was Jehoshaphat trying to fulfill by sending out his officials?

2 Chronicles 17:10-13. Describe Judah's situation under the reign of Jehoshaphat.

2. Read 2 Chronicles 20.

Fear Factor

Saul. David. Solomon—kings who reigned over a united Israel. But after Solomon's death the kingdom divided. North and South, Israel and Judah, respectively. And of all the kings of Israel and Judah, only eight pleased the Lord. Jehoshaphat probably was one of the most godly kings of Judah. Don't misunderstand me; he wasn't perfect. He made some incredibly stupid mistakes along the way that had lasting effects on his legacy. However, this week we'll concentrate on the more positive aspects of Jehoshaphat's life.

We learn from 2 Chronicles 17:6 that Jehoshaphat's heart "was devoted to the ways of the LORD." In other words, he desired to please God. He sought God. He followed God's commands. He recognized God as the one true God and did not seek the false gods the Canaanites served (2 Chronicles 17:3, 4). He knew God and wanted others to know him as well, so he established an education program to teach the people of Judah the Book of the Law—all the commandments of Moses (Joshua 1:7, 8). The result? "The LORD was with Jehoshaphat" (2 Chronicles 17:3). All the kingdoms in the lands surrounding Judah did not make war against Jehoshaphat because "the dread of the LORD" (*NASB*) was on them (v. 10). The Philistines and Arabians brought gifts to him (v. 11), and Jehoshaphat's kingdom grew greater and greater. He had fortresses and supply cities, warriors and valiant men. His troops numbered more than one million (vv. 14-19)! Great honor and riches were his, yet he still "set [his] heart on seeking God" (2 Chronicles 19:3).

That's the big picture of Jehoshaphat, but what about in the daily grind? How did he live out his faith day to day? We are privileged to get a glimpse of this man in action in 2 Chronicles 20.

Jehoshaphat felt a sense of security in his world. He was amassing riches, receiving honor, training his army—life was good. Then from out of nowhere came a bad report. A military coalition of enemy nations was mounting an attack. Already in Judah's territory, the encroachment rapidly advanced. Jehoshaphat's reaction? Fear.

I can relate. I have experienced my own world turning upside down.

I was on my cell phone chatting with my friend Tonya. We covered the basics—from our current hair color to our kids' latest antics. Everything for both of us was going great. Life was good. In the midst of this "deep" conversation, I heard my husband answer a phone call from my mom. Soon Ron came into the room where I was and said, "Your dad has had a major stroke."

Bam! My dad . . . our family's rock, our strength and stability, suddenly was completely paralyzed on his entire left side. This pillar of a man was unable to walk. This articulate man was stuttering . . . mumbling . . . drooling. My reaction? Fear.

Has your world ever turned upside down?

●● The doctor calls—the diagnosis is cancer.

●● Your company informs you they are closing their doors. Unemployment stares you in the face.

•• The baby in your womb has died.

•• You find out your suspicions are true—your spouse is having an affair.

•• Your son tells you that he is in love—with another man.

You cannot breathe. A legion of chaotic thoughts assaults you. You're afraid.

To react with fear is perfectly normal given the circumstances. But what do you do with that fear? Wallow in it? Allow your mind to go down the paths of despair and defeat? Think constantly about the horrible situation in which you find yourself?

Do you become totally consumed by fear? Or do you respond like Jehoshaphat?

The *New American Standard Bible* says it like this: "And Jehoshaphat was afraid and turned his attention to seek the LORD" (2 Chronicles 20:3).

······ •◉• ······

DAY TWO: READ
The Battle Plan

In 2 Chronicles 20 Jehoshaphat shows us a four-step battle plan we can use against the debilitating enemy of fear.

Step 1. Seek the Lord.
Based on 2 Chronicles 20, write a quick assessment of the problem facing Jehoshaphat.

What was Jehoshaphat's emotional reaction?

According to verse 3, what did Jehoshaphat do?

In seeking the Lord, Jehoshaphat led the people of Judah in prayer. Analyze Jehoshaphat's prayer. On what attributes of God does Jehoshaphat focus (vv. 6-9)?

Define the problems Jehoshaphat sees (vv. 10-12).

Step 2. Stand before the Lord.
According to 2 Chronicles 20:13, who was standing before the Lord?

What were they waiting for? Did they get it?

What was the answer?

Step 3. Sing to the Lord.
Look again at 2 Chronicles 20:15-17. What was the battle plan?

What specific marching orders did Jehoshaphat give (vv. 20, 21)?

How did he position the people of Jerusalem and Judah for battle?

According to verses 22, 23, what happened when the men began singing and praising God?

Step 4. See the salvation of the Lord.

What did the men of Judah see when they came to the overlook (vv. 24-26)?

How long did it take them to gather the plunder from the battle?

What did they do after they gathered the plunder?

The Strategy

The scenario: King Jehoshaphat had just received word that several enemies had allied themselves to make war against him. This massive military alliance had already crossed Judah's border. How did Jehoshaphat handle the news? Let's take a look at his response and the life lessons we can learn from J-E-H . . . O-S-H . . . A-P-H-A-T. The lessons match the four steps of Jehoshaphat's battle plan.

Lesson 1: Seek the Lord

With the enemy advancing toward Jerusalem, how did Jehoshaphat turn from his fear? He did it by seeking the Lord through prayer. No kidding! Three enemy nations united together breathing down his neck, and he called a prayer meeting. We might think a planning session with his joint chiefs of staff would have been more practical. Instead, Jehoshaphat gathered all of Judah and prayed. His prayer offers us insight on how to seek God.

Jehoshaphat recognized God as God. Right from the start, Jehoshaphat kept his focus and attention on God. He prayed, "O LORD, God of our fathers, are you not the God who is in heaven? You rule over all the kingdoms of the nations. Power and might are in your hand, and no one can withstand you" (2 Chronicles 20:6).

God. The one true God. The one and *only* God. The creator of the heavens and the earth. The ruler of all nations. The God who establishes and rules over all kingdoms. *God*—the powerful. *God*—the Almighty. The in-control God. The ultimate-authority God. Jehoshaphat knew this God and recognized him before all of Judah.

Do you recognize God as God? What kind of verbal tribute do you give him?

King David wrote, "I sought the LORD, and he answered me; he delivered me from all my fears" (Psalm 34:4). Seeking God in fearful situations is vital. Seeking God is the antidote to fear. By taking our eyes off ourselves and our circumstances and focusing on the one who created us and holds all things together (Colossians 1:17), we can know peace. Jehoshaphat kept his eyes and the eyes of the people of Judah on the one who could deliver them. He first sought God by recognizing who God is.

Jehoshaphat recognized what God had done. A proven track record holds up when others challenge it. It lasts. It endures. You can count on it. And God has one, a track record like none other. Challenged and tested for thousands of years, and yet he holds true. He is the same "yesterday and today and forever" (Hebrews 13:8, *NASB*). Jehoshaphat recognized that God does not change and that the miraculous things he had done in the past for his people were possible for Judah as well: "O our God, did you not drive out the inhabitants of this land before your people Israel and give it forever to the descendants of Abraham your friend? They have lived in it and have built in it a sanctuary for your Name" (2 Chronicles 20:7, 8).

During our study of Achan, we learned that God drove out the inhabitants of Canaan and gave the land to the Israelites. Remember Jericho, the first city God allowed Israel to conquer? The Lord told the Israelites to march around that walled city seven days in a row and on the seventh day to give a great shout. The Israelites obeyed, and when they gave their shout, the walls came tumbling down (Joshua 6:20). God was Israel's warrior, and although his methods were extremely unorthodox, they were also exceedingly effective! This was the first of many victories God gave Israel. City after city succumbed.

Usually the Israelites were outnumbered by their enemies and often they lacked equipment. Didn't matter. God was faithful and performed great wonders on behalf of his people. Jehoshaphat remembered these things and recounted God's actions for the people of Judah. In doing this he reminded them of God's faithfulness.

We can do the same. How many times has God shown himself to be faithful in your own life? What miracle has he performed for you . . . big or small?

- Peace and comfort came that no doctor or medicine could provide.

- Doors opened on a new opportunity.

- Joy replaced jealousy and you truly celebrated a friend's good news.

- Your marriage was renewed and restored.

- Someone spoke words of encouragement when you desperately needed them.

Remember what God has done. Recount his faithfulness to others. He never changes. You can count on him. He has a proven track record.

Jehoshaphat recognized God as promise keeper. D. L. Moody is credited with saying, "Tarry at a promise and God will meet you there." Jehoshaphat knew the promises of God. He knew that God makes good on his word. Jehoshaphat determined to meet God at a specific promise and have all of Judah participate with him. Specifically, Jehoshaphat knew God would deliver Israel's enemies if Israel would stand before God and cry out to him (2 Chronicles 6:20, 28-30, 34, 35; Psalm 50:15; 91:15). In his prayer he recounted that promise and gathered the people of Judah together to cry out to God. Jehoshaphat knew God had promised—therefore, God would deliver.

How confident are you in God as promise keeper? Do you know the promises well enough to tarry at them? Have you ever looked at the promises of God—I mean really

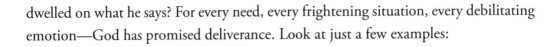

dwelled on what he says? For every need, every frightening situation, every debilitating emotion—God has promised deliverance. Look at just a few examples:

. . . .

He gives strength to the weary and increases the power of the weak. (Isaiah 40:29)

He who began a good work in you will carry it on to completion. (Philippians 1:6)

As far as the east is from the west, so far has he removed our transgressions from us. (Psalm 103:12)

. . . .

Jehoshaphat led his people to cry out before the Lord, seeking his deliverance. They tarried at his promise, and God was preparing to meet them there . . . at the crossroads of deliverance!

Jehoshaphat recognized God as the source of wisdom. As I'm writing this, our nation is entering an election year. Politicians are amping up their campaigns, messages, and platforms. Everyone running for office has a plan—a plan to balance the budget, control inflation, secure the border, fix Social Security, eliminate debt, win the war on terror, create more jobs, improve education, save the environment—and on and on it goes. Surely no politician can know how to do *all* these things; neither can anyone's plans be 100 percent effective. All we have to do is look at history to figure that one out! But have you ever heard anyone running for office or anyone in government say, "I have no idea how to deal with that issue" or "I don't know what to do"?

Well, Jehoshaphat didn't know what to do, and he did say those very words: "For we have no power to face this vast army that is attacking us. We do not know what to do" (2 Chronicles 20:12). He recognized *and* verbalized, before all of Judah, his cluelessness! But he knew God was not clueless. So he turned his attention and his eyes to the one who is the source of all wisdom (Proverbs 2:6; Romans 11:33).

How brilliant, and how uncommon as well! Let's be honest here. Most of us, when faced with a crisis, try to figure our own way out. We plan; we groan; we agonize. We seek others' opinions, read, search the Internet—all in pursuit of wisdom. Yet we neglect going to the *source* of wisdom—God himself. James 1:2, 5 says that when we lack wisdom in the midst of trials, we are to ask of God, who will not only give wisdom but dole it out generously!

Jehoshaphat teaches us a very valuable lesson here: go to God first. Seek out his wisdom and his plan. The result: he will show us that plan.

Lesson 2: Stand Before the Lord

Jehoshaphat prayed to God before all the people of Judah, seeking wisdom for handling the situation with the rapidly approaching enemy army. We read that after Jehoshaphat prayed, all the people "stood there before the LORD" (2 Chronicles 20:13). Why? They were waiting for God to respond!

Waiting on God. We live in an instant society—everything happens fast. Instant coffee—no brewing necessary. Instant messaging—talk online anytime. Instant replay—an immediate second look at critical sports plays. Fast food—prepared and packaged, ready for you to order. Even quick-fix boxed macaroni and cheese can be made more quickly now—pop it in the microwave and it's ready in seconds!

Given that we live in such a fast-paced, immediate-results world, I have been amazed at how much waiting my life requires. I have come to the conclusion that waiting is my lot in life . . . because I wait a lot in life! I wait for my kids—at the orthodontist's office, at softball practice, soccer practice, guitar lessons, at school. I'll pop in to my husband's office to say hello or join him for lunch and have to wait for patients to be seen and charts to be finished. I wait in line at the grocery store—and inevitably the person in front of me will need a price check on an item from the opposite side of the store! I even wait for my "fast food," pulling over into a parking space to wait until someone can bring it to me.

Having been raised to be productive, I put together a basket of items to carry with me for such times. I have options. I can either read, crochet, or knit!

But when God asks me to wait? My productivity instinct kicks in and says I need to *do* something, *produce* something, *accomplish* something. God, however, asks me to wait, and in that waiting, to rest. To let go and let God handle the situation.

. . . .

Be still, and know that I am God. (Psalm 46:10)

My soul, wait in silence for God only,
For my hope is from Him. (Psalm 62:5, *NASB*)

I waited patiently for the LORD;
he turned to me and heard my cry. (Psalm 40:1)

. . . .

King Jehoshaphat and all the people of Judah waited on God. They stood silently, expectantly, waiting for God's guidance. What about you? Are you silent or striving? Are you hopeful or fearful? Are you patient or frantic? Take a lesson from Jehoshaphat: wait . . . and know that God will give you a word.

A word from God. "How do you know when God is speaking to you?" Several students asked this question when my husband and I led the college ministry at our church. It's a great question! How *do* we know?

Jehoshaphat and the people waited for a response from God—and God gave them one through a man named Jahaziel. "Do not be afraid or discouraged because of this vast army. For the battle is not yours, but God's. Tomorrow march down against them. . . . You will not have to fight this battle. Take up your positions; stand firm and see the deliverance the LORD will give you, O Judah and Jerusalem. Do not be afraid; do not be discouraged. Go out to face them tomorrow, and the LORD will be with you" (2 Chronicles 20:15-17).

Judah would not have to fight this battle; God said he would do it! This news could have seemed disconcerting given the well-equipped enemy army ready to pounce. So how did Jehoshaphat know with certainty this message was from God? Because it was consistent with the covenant-keeping God whom Jehoshaphat sought after and followed.

The same principle holds true for you and me: we can know the message is God's if it is consistent with his character and his Word.

Remember, Jehoshaphat had implemented a religious education program throughout the land so the people would know the Book of the Law. The people had learned God's character and message as a result of this program. Knowing these, they recognized God's Word when it was spoken to them. He told them the battle was his. Jehoshaphat knew this message was from God because it was consistent with Scripture.

Jehoshaphat knew the message was consistent with God's character too. His father, Asa, had faced a similar situation years before. The Ethiopians, who outnumbered Asa's troops nearly two to one, came against him in war. Asa, a man who sought God, called upon God to save the people of Judah. And God did. The Lord fought the battle for Asa that day and gave great victory to the people of Judah (2 Chronicles 14:1-15). I can imagine that Asa shared this story with his son Jehoshaphat and that his testimony of God's power aided Jehoshaphat's faith.

> ## OBSCURE
> ### Bible Facts
> Jahaziel, whom the Spirit of the Lord came upon to deliver the message to Jehoshaphat, was a descendant of Asaph, a writer of several Psalms. Some believe Jahaziel may have followed in his forefather's footsteps and written Psalm 83, to commemorate this victory.

Is God speaking to you? You can know with certainty if the message you hear lines up with God's character and his Word. Whatever battle you are facing, take a lesson from Jehoshaphat: Fear not! The battle belongs to the Lord!

Lesson 3: Sing to the Lord

If I could ask God for one talent, it would be to sing. I cannot carry a tune in a bucket. Oh, I try . . . ask anyone driving next to me on the highway. That's my favorite place to *pretend* I can sing—in my car, all alone, with the windows up and the radio blaring—so I don't even have to listen to myself. Yup, I'd love to be able to sing.

If I were living during the day of Jehoshaphat, though, I might want to rethink that wish, for Jehoshaphat used his singers in an unconventional way.

Think about the scene: Jehoshaphat and the people of Judah had sought the Lord regarding the encroaching enemy, waited for God to give them an answer, and heard through a prophet that God would fight the battle for them. The army was to march out to face the enemy, but they were to let the Lord do the fighting.

So where do the singers come in? Well, the morning of the battle, Jehoshaphat gave everyone a pep talk. He reminded them that success would come when they put their trust in God. He then positioned the singers, the priests, and the army. The unconventional part? He placed the singers *in front of* the army! Could it be that Jehoshaphat understood that by doing this, he revealed his true faith? Psalm 20:7 says, "Some trust in chariots and some in horses, but we trust in the name of the LORD our God." What an incredible way to show trust in God . . . by praising him through song!

What are your circumstances? Are you facing a daunting enemy? Would you feel more confident if you had trained individuals around you, ready to ward off any advance from the evil one? Sometimes God uses the most unlikely characters and circumstances to stretch our faith. Jehoshaphat knew his singers were not going to bring the victory. Judah's strength was not in the musicians but in God, yet through the musicians God heard and saw Judah's faith and acted on their behalf. "As they began to sing and praise, the LORD set ambushes against the men of Ammon and Moab and Mount Seir who were invading Judah, and they were defeated" (2 Chronicles 20:22).

What is God hearing from you? Is it a song of praise even in the midst of trials? If so, keep singing, child of God! Keep singing and see the salvation of the Lord!

Lesson 4: See the Salvation of the Lord

"You will not have to fight this battle. Take up your positions; stand firm and see the deliverance the LORD will give you" (2 Chronicles 20:17).

In the archives of *The New Yorker* magazine, I found an article about an Oklahoma man who had been blind for forty-five years when doctors performed surgery on his eyes. Although the surgery restored Virgil's vision, Virgil never really understood what he was seeing unless he was able to touch it. "Virgil's behavior was . . . the behavior of one *mentally* blind, or agnosic—able to see but not to decipher what he was seeing."[30]

As I read, I found myself feeling sorry for Virgil. Imagine having your eyes wide open and stimuli making its way to your brain yet having no understanding of what you are seeing! Then I realized . . . I am—and perhaps you are—very much like Virgil. In a spiritual sense agnosia might be an epidemic! For God continually works, but we so often are blind to his activity. Our eyes receive the stimuli, but our brains do not recognize God doing the great things around us. Time and again we pass it off as coincidence, good luck, a fluke in nature, a scientific advance. We are spiritual agnosics.

A family from a church we attended years ago had a son with Fragile X syndrome, a form of mental retardation. During the conservative-style worship service, this boy raised his hands up in the air and clapped loudly at seemingly inappropriate times. He giggled and shouted praises to God and constantly had a smile on his face. His mother knew a few in the congregation viewed her son as a distraction. Giving a devotional one evening, she talked about our expressions of worship. The room was deafeningly silent when she left us with a final question: "When God sees us worshipping him, whom do you think he views as the retarded ones?"

We have things backward, don't we?

Jehoshaphat didn't. He and all of Judah share a wonderful life lesson with us as the scene in 2 Chronicles 20 comes to an end. They went out to the battlefield in obedience to God's promise and saw that God had indeed done the fighting for them. The enemy armies had utterly destroyed one another! They were all corpses. Judah didn't have to raise a weapon in combat. Not only did God fight for them but he also gave them an abundance of plunder, so much that it took three days to carry away all the goods.

Recognizing that the victory was from God, the people of Judah assembled together to give thanks to him for all the blessings he bestowed on them. No spiritual agnosia here. No retardation in this worship. The lesson: open your eyes . . . see and decipher that God is at work in your life!

DAY THREE: RELATE
Power from Above

Look at this verse: "For God has not given us a spirit of fear and timidity, but of power, love, and self-discipline" (2 Timothy 1:7, *NLT*).

God does not want us to be overcome by our fear. He wants to give us victory instead. The battle plan, then, must be focused on the power that comes from him. Jehoshaphat's four-step plan does just that. Let's stick with his strategy for dealing with fear and look up several cross-references that support this plan. Write what you learn as you read each verse.

Step 1. Seek the Lord.
Psalm 34:4

James 1:5

Hebrews 13:8

Step 2. Stand before the Lord.
Psalm 46:10

Psalm 62:5

Psalm 40:1

Step 3. Sing to the Lord.
Psalm 20:7

Psalm 149

Ephesians 5:19

Step 4. See the salvation of the Lord.
Ephesians 1:18, 19

Acts 26:15-18

DAY FOUR: REFLECT
Facing Your Fears

Jehoshaphat lived in a different time and culture than ours, but his problem is very current. I'm sure you have faced fearful situations many times too. Today I want you to think about how you typically handle fear and then determine if you need to implement a new strategy.

1. Think of a circumstance that made you fearful. How did you face it? To whom or what did you turn?

2. What is your first response in a fearful situation? Some of us cry. Others scream. Still others internalize their concern and jeopardize their health. Maybe you pick up the phone and call friends or family. Maybe you search the Internet for information or answers. Maybe you eat, drink, shop, sleep, or take medicine. Whatever your strategy, it might be time to set up a new game plan. By way of reminder, write out the four steps Jehoshaphat used to face his fears.

3. Spend time with God.

   List at least three situations that God has helped you through. Praise him for who he is and what he has already done in your life.

   Write out a battle that is looming large in your life right now. In prayer, ask God to take what you have written. Surrender that situation to him.

Seek God's wisdom. Ask him to show you how to implement his battle plan and give you eyes to see his salvation.

Spend time being still and listening to God. If the Holy Spirit impresses you with a verse, a phrase, or a thought, write it here.

Listen to your favorite music that you use to worship. Sing along, play along, or simply listen with an attitude of worship and offer your thoughts as a sacrifice of praise to your heavenly Father.

DAY FIVE: REMEMBER
The Battle Belongs to the Lord

Knowing the Word is vital when we face battles. God can use the Scripture we've hidden in our hearts to direct us and give us peace.

1. Once again, choose a verse to memorize from this week's study. Write it out and share it aloud with friends and family. Review the verses you've worked on in previous weeks too.

2. Add to your list or chart regarding all that you've learned about God through this week's lesson. When you are struggling because of the battles that rage around you, pull out your list and praise God for each of the attributes you have noted. Your burden will feel much lighter when you realize your battle is in the capable hands of Almighty God!

God's Victory

Remember when I told you about my dad's stroke? We thought we lost him that day . . . either to death or to paralysis. But God fought that battle for us, and Dad walked out of the hospital without assistance. That was in February 2003. Evidently, my heavenly Father had plans yet for my earthly father. Dad understood this and shared his miraculous story with many, fully attributing the victory to God. He has seen friends come to know Jesus as a result.

Like Jehoshaphat, our family walked through a fearful time. We learned that in the midst of trials our first response should be to turn our attention to the Lord. When we seek him, stand and wait on him, and sing his praises, we can be assured that we will see his salvation.

Thanks for the life lessons, King Jehoshaphat!

OBSCURE OBSERVATIONS

It isn't that Christianity has been tried and found wanting. It is that it has been found difficult and so never really tried. —G. K. Chesterton

amos:
a blue-collar guy

MOVING OUT OF YOUR COMFORT ZONE • THE BOOK OF AMOS

Out of My League!

American icons and presidents have enjoyed the luxurious amenities and exquisite views of The Grove Park Inn, one of the South's most famous resorts and spas. Nestled in the Blue Ridge Mountains of North Carolina, the resort also boasts a world-renowned spa. From mineral pools with underwater music to waterfall and contrast pools, this spa has it all. Forty-three-thousand square feet of pure decadence built with an elegance and sophistication few can rival. And I got to go there!

My husband signed up for a continuing education course offered at the Inn—three days, two nights, spouses welcome. Woo-hoo! I made a reservation for the spa's least expensive offering, a pedicure, something that wouldn't totally bust my budget. As part of my appointment, I had the the opportunity to enjoy a full day in the spa's facility.

We arrived later than anticipated, so my spa hours would be shortened. Wanting to make the most of the remaining time, I left Ron to do the checking in while I grabbed my bag and headed to the soothing, subterranean facility. I'd never been to a spa before, and I knew this first experience would be unforgettable!

The spa concierge ushered me back to the women's changing room, where I was given a plush robe and slippers. Unfortunately, my late arrival left only men's extra-large sizes available. Needless to say, the robe was a bit cumbersome on my medium frame, and the slippers made me feel as if I were five years old, slinking around in my dad's size 13s! I schlepped through the women's relaxation room and out to the pool area, where I ditched the robe and slippers and plunged into the mineral pool.

With underwater music, the pool was divine, but after a few minutes of frolicking in the enriched water, I noticed I was the only one by myself. Everyone else was a couple. I began to miss Ron. Well, maybe I could spot him on the golf course. So I headed to the oversized outdoor whirlpool that looked out on the pristine greens.

Ahh. Much better. The warm water soothed the subtle bubblings of inferiority, and with a more diverse group around me, I began to relax. Unfortunately, I don't handle heat too well, and the warm water quickly became overwhelming. So I decided to sit on the side of the pool, get some fresh air, and enjoy the view. I pushed myself up out of the pool and turned to sit on the cement decking.

A horrifying thing happened. An air pocket formed between my thighs and the concrete and a noise erupted—you know, the kind of noise a squeezable ketchup bottle makes when it's running out of ketchup? That's what everyone around me heard!

Mortified, I began to explain, "That wasn't me! It was an air pocket. Really, it was! I didn't make that noise!"

A sweet southern lady responded, "Honey, it's OK. We all make that sound every now and again."

"No. You don't understand! I didn't make *that* sound! Well, I did, but it wasn't me; it was the wet concrete and this air pocket, and . . ." The longer I tried to explain the science behind the sound, the more second-class I sounded. I had to get out of there!

Back inside I saw the waterfall pools. That's what I needed! The waterfall pools were supposed to de-stress. Another patron was standing under the falls, enjoying the benefits of the thousands of gallons of water streaming on his back. "Would you like to try this?" he asked.

"Absolutely," I said with a smile. "I really could use a de-stresser about now."

He moved and stood behind me. Not quite knowing where I wanted the water to fall, I eased myself under its surge. Before I knew it, the water came plunging down and took with it my tankini bottoms! There I stood, in all my glory, with a kind stranger gawking at me from behind—or should I say gawking *at* my behind? Mortified once again!

I'd had enough. I just wanted a shower and to get ready for my pedicure. So that's what I did. But . . . I forgot my towel. Being an overly modest person, this presented a problem. *Think, LeAnne, think!* Aha! I'd just put my wet bathing suit back on and head to the dressing room. Which I did. I met a couple of ladies along the route and had a wonderful conversation with one in particular. But when I got to my dressing room and closed the door, I looked in the full-length mirror and shrieked—my bathing suit was *inside out*—my *black* bathing suit with a *tan* lining! Ugh.

I told the pedicurist to please hurry up. Then I ran to our hotel room.

Ron arrived an hour later, fully satisfied with his experience on the links, and asked, "How was your spa day?"

I burst into tears. "I don't belong here! I'm out of my league!"

Have you ever felt as if you didn't fit in? Weren't qualified? Lacked the right credentials?

Welcome to Amos's world! A shepherd from the south who also did a little fig farming on the side, Amos didn't have the most prestigious career. (It probably compared to a modern-day garbage collector. Extremely valuable *to* society yet not enormously valued *by* society.) Nonetheless, Amos was God's man, called on for a special assignment. And Amos understood that when God calls, you answer!

"Amos."

"Yes, God?"

"I have a job for you."

"Me?"

"Yes, you."

"What do you want me to do?"

"I need you to deliver a message to the northern kingdom."

"A message? God, I'm not a messenger. I'm a fig farmer, remember? And besides that, I live in the *southern* kingdom!"

"I am very aware of that, Amos. But you're the man I want for this job!"

"I'm not so sure about this, God. . . . But you *are* God, so I guess I need to go with it. What kind of message do you want me to deliver? Who's it going to?"

"Simple. I just want you to go to the two highest officials in Israel, King Jeroboam II and Amaziah, the high priest. Tell them that they and the people of the northern kingdom are a bunch of hypocritical, obstinate, unjust, immoral, idolatrous, self-serving, gluttonous cows, and I've had it with them—destruction is imminent!"

"O-K, God. N-n-no problem. (Gulp!)"

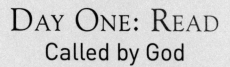

DAY ONE: READ
Called by God

Amos was one of the *minor prophets* (called so because their writings are short; Amos's book in the Old Testament book has just nine chapters), but his message to Israel was major! We'll not be able to dig into all nine chapters here, but we'll take a close look at smaller portions of the book.

In order to get a feel for the big picture, however, first read the entire book in one sitting. Choose a version of the Bible that's easy to read and understand. Before you begin, ask God to open your eyes, your ears, and your heart to his message.

1. After you have read Amos 1–9, write out your first impressions here.

2. When studying a book of the Bible, we can learn much about the author by reading the text itself. Read Amos 1:1; 7:14, 15.

   Where was Amos from?

What was his occupation?

What did the Lord commission Amos to do?

3. God called Amos to *prophesy* (to deliver a message about the future) to Israel—but Amos was from Tekoa, in Judah. (At this point in Israel's history, the nation was divided. Judah was the southern kingdom, Israel the northern.)

Read 1 Kings 11:9-13 to learn why the kingdom was divided. Write out the reason below.

Why might this have been an issue for Amos to overcome?

DAY TWO: READ
Called on the Carpet

Amos's job was to go to the northern kingdom of Israel and pronounce condemnation and the coming judgment.

1. Read Amos 2:6-8. Why was Israel being condemned?

2. Read the following passages from Amos 4 and answer the questions:

   Verses 1-3. The well-fed cattle raised in Bashan were considered the best breed in ancient Canaan. But verse 1 is not referring to literal cows. Who might Amos be addressing here?

   What attitude or sin is he pointing out?

Verses 4, 5. When the kingdom divided, Jeroboam I became king of Israel. Because he feared the Israelites might defect to Judah when they went to worship at the temple in Jerusalem, he devised his own religious system. He commissioned his own priests and his own feasts. He set up places of worship at Bethel and Dan and declared them holy. He encouraged the people to use these places to present their sacrifices and offerings to God. All this, of course, was contrary to the ways God had established for his people.

Knowing this history, reread verses 4, 5. What two places are high-lighted in these verses?

What was being done at these places?

What kind of tone do you sense when reading these verses?

What sin is Amos denouncing?

Verses 6-13. What specific things did God do to get Israel's attention?

What general sin do these verses highlight?

3. Amos began his prophecy by saying, "The LORD roars from Zion" (1:2). In other words, he wanted to make sure that Israel knew God meant business. After condemning the Israelites of their many sins, Amos pronounced God's judgment. Read Amos 3:11-15; 6:14. What was the judgment God intended to administer?

4. The nation God used to dole out his punishment was Assyria, a nation just beginning to gain power when Amos was prophesying. Calculate the number of years from the time Amos began prophesying (750 BC) until Israel was taken into captivity by Assyria (722 BC). How many years would it be before Amos's prophecies would become reality?

A Wake-Up Call

Amos the southern fig-farming shepherd actually followed through on his assignment. He identified and elaborated on the sinful actions and attitudes the Israelites exhibited. Oddly enough, these don't seem too far off from our own world. Hmm . . .

Injustice

As the youngest of three, I often played the injustice card when my older siblings seemed to get more privileges than me. "That's not fair!" I whined. Now as a mom I hear that same phrase all too often. And like every other mom across America, I respond, "Get used to it, sweetie, because life isn't always fair."

Yet injustice in God's eyes is much more than squabbling siblings and standardized comebacks. It is deep. It is serious. It devalues those whom God created, and it goes to the core of who and what God is. Psalm 89:14 tells us that "righteousness and justice are the foundation of [God's] throne." Being God's messenger, Amos rightfully called the people of Israel out on their unjust ways—crushing the needy and exploiting the poverty stricken (Amos 4:1; 5:11, 12; 8:4), denying justice to the oppressed and selling the poor (Amos 2:6, 7)—all very grave offenses in the eyes of a very just God.

We see injustices all around us today as well, from the killing of innocent babies in the womb to worldwide sex trafficking to millions of people held in bonded slavery.[31] God's heart must be breaking now as it was then.

Immorality

Embarrassed, I turned red as a beet. A completely innocent viewing of a Super Bowl halftime show ended up being the talk of our college ministry group, not to mention the talk of the nation, for weeks on end. You remember it too, I'm sure—Justin Timberlake, Janet Jackson, and the infamous "wardrobe malfunction." Yet as a nation we already have moved on to more tantalizing fare. *Sexting*, sending nude pictures via cell phone, seems to be the newest craze for indecent exposure. This doesn't even begin to touch on the extent of sexual promiscuity among teens, partner swapping among married couples, or sexual perversion and homosexual lifestyles. Lewd and unchaste behavior is rampant today.

So it was in Amos's day. One of the messages he shared with Israel was condemnation for sexual immorality. Fathers and sons were sleeping with the same women!

God expected his people to behave differently—to be *holy*, which means "set apart." "For you are a people holy to the LORD your God" (Deuteronomy 7:6). He gave them the law so they would know what sin looked like. He inspired them by promising blessings for obedience. He gave a clear description of the curses that would befall them if they didn't follow his ways.

And he expects the same of us: "Be holy because I am holy" (1 Peter 1:15). Don't embrace today's norms, but "flee from sexual immorality" (1 Corinthians 6:18). Be a person set apart for God! "You are the light of the world" (Matthew 5:14).

Idolatry

If you looked at my checkbook register and my calendar, I'll bet you could discern fairly accurately where my priorities lie, both good and bad. What if I looked at yours? Would I be able to determine the most important people and things in your life? Are God and his agenda evident through you, or are there idols at play?

You might protest, "But I don't have any little Buddha figurines in my house that I pray to!"

Idols don't have to come in the form of pudgy, shirtless bald men.

Louie Giglio, in a video series called *Worship: That Thing We Do*,[32] paints a word picture of idolatry that might help clarify. He says each of us has a throne and on that throne sits what or whom we worship. For some it truly is God. For others it's their children. Still others worship their jobs, favorite sports teams, the latest fashions, or the ideal of a perfectly fit body. There's also a trail leading to that throne with clues that tell us who or what is currently perched there. The way we use our time, treasure, and talents are all clues about whatever we hold in high esteem—the things or ones we worship. According to Giglio, everyone worships something.

Israel left clues, blatant clues. The people offered sacrifices to pagan gods and slept with prostitutes in the temples of false gods (Amos 2:7, 8). The Israelites didn't have God on their throne: "You have lifted up the shrine of your king, the pedestal of your idols, the star of your god—which you made for yourselves" (Amos 5:26).

God had made it perfectly clear that he was the one and only God and the only one to be worshipped:

. . . .

I am the LORD; that is my name! I will not give my glory to another or my praise to idols. (Isaiah 42:8)

I am God, and there is no other; I am God, and there is none like me. (Isaiah 46:9)

You shall have no other gods before me. You shall not make for yourself an idol. . . . You shall not bow down to them or worship them; for I, the LORD your God, am a jealous God. (Exodus 20:3-5)

. . . .

Pefectly clear, wouldn't you say? Then why do we have such a hard time hearing it ourselves?

Luxury

"When I get a daily massage, then I'll know I've arrived!" Little did this servant of God realize that she would indeed *arrive*—as a missionary in Mexico. The mission organization had a volunteer on site who offered daily massages for the staff. What a sense of humor God has! What extravagance he provides.

Luxury. Its definition varies from country to country and culture to culture, and its recipients vary in their reaction to it. We know that "every good and perfect gift is from above" (James 1:17) and that God himself made Abraham, David, and Solomon some of the wealthiest men ever to walk the earth. So what's the problem? Why did Amos speak against the luxurious lifestyles of those in the northern kingdom?

Because living *in* luxury is one thing, but living *for* luxury is another.

The people were said to be "at ease" (Amos 6:1, *NASB*), reclining on opulent beds made of ivory, sprawling out on their couches, eating lambs and calves and drinking wine from bowls. They enjoyed beautiful music and expensive perfumes (vv. 4-6). They had summer houses and winter houses (Amos 3:15) and fattened themselves with all their abundance (4:1). The problem? These luxuries distracted the people and kept their focus from the evils in their land. Amos said, "You do not grieve over the ruin of Joseph" (6:6). Too busy partying and playing Bunko to recognize the shambles their country had come to!

Hypocrisy

In ancient Greek theaters actors wore masks to depict various characters and emotions.[33] In the Greek language the word for *actor, stage player*, and *pretender* was *hypokrites*.[34] Our English language maintains the same meaning and nearly the same spelling, for the word *hypocrite* describes a pretender or one who wears a mask.

Although *hypocritical* and its Greek origin came long after Amos's day, the word aptly defines the people in the northern kingdom playacting their religious activities. These pretenders even wanted everyone to see what they were doing, as if they would receive applause for their performance.

The audience of one for whom they should have been performing was not pleased. He didn't appreciate that they were worshipping at a false temple set up by false priests and completely neglecting the proper way to present their sacrifices and offerings. They loved their cultural religious festivities, but they didn't love the God they claimed to worship. Their hearts were far from him (Isaiah 29:13). It's an ongoing symptom of a hypocritical people.

What masks are we wearing? For what religious activities might we be seeking the world's applause? Shouldn't we be seeking the approval and the applause of the one who matters? Maybe it's time to take off our masks and get real . . . with ourselves and especially with God.

Stubbornness

When I want to get my point across, I repeat myself. When I want to get my point across, I repeat myself. I think God uses that same approach. (Although I got the idea from him, not vice versa!) Five times in six verses, he says, "Yet you have not returned to me" (Amos 4:6, 8, 9, 10, 11) to show the people of Israel how absolutely obstinate they were.

God used drastic measures to get the attention of the Israelites so they would repent and come back to him. He sent famine, drought, crop-destroying insects, plagues, defeat in war . . . yet they did not return to him.

What measures has God taken in my life in order to get my attention? Did the promotion or the pink slip turn my eyes upward? What about the diagnosis or the deliverance? Has God been trying to get our attention as a nation? Could terrorism, natural disasters, or the collapse of our economy be used by God to shake us up?

Make no mistake, he wants us to turn to him. He longs to eternally bless us with a deep, intimate relationship with him. Let's not be like the people of Israel and turn our backs on him yet again.

···

DAY THREE: RELATE
Least Likely to Succeed

Remember that in this phase of inductive study, we want to relate to the author and to the whole counsel of Scripture.

1. Our author, Amos, worked as a shepherd and a farmer—not the most respected occupations during Bible times. Yet God called him to go to the upper echelon of Israel's society to proclaim his message. Amos delivered that message in Bethel. He spoke directly to Amaziah the priest, who reported his words to King Jeroboam II (Amos 7:10-13).

This is not the first time in Scripture that we have seen God use unlikely people to carry out huge tasks. In the list that follows, I've described the tasks some of these unlikely ones accomplished. Look up the verses and find the part of each person's resume that would have put him or her in the least-likely-to-succeed category.

Nehemiah's accomplishment: Led a group of former exiles to rebuild the wall around Jerusalem.

Least likely to succeed because (Nehemiah 1:11):

Jesus' disciples' accomplishment: Brought worldwide revolution by sharing the gospel message of Jesus Christ. Least likely to succeed because:

Mark 1:16

Mark 1:19

Luke 5:27

Luke 6:15

Rahab's accomplishments: Aided Israel by hiding spies in her home in the wall of Jericho; listed in the genealogy of Jesus.

Least likely to succeed because (Joshua 2:1):

Jephthah's accomplishment: Delivered Israel from the Ammonites.

Least likely to succeed because (Judges 11:1):

2. Who exactly were the Israelites, and how did God feel about them? Look up the following verses and write a description from each passage:

Exodus 1:7

Exodus 4:22

Exodus 32:13

Deuteronomy 26:17-19

Isaiah 43:1-3

Jeremiah 31:3

Romans 9:4, 5

3. Why would God set the Israelites apart to be his people? What purpose can you see in each of the following verses? Do we, as Christ followers, have that same purpose?

Israelites: Deuteronomy 28:9, 10

Christ followers: 1 Peter 2:9, 12

Israelites: Genesis 12:1-3

Christ followers: Galatians 3:8

Israelites: Genesis 15:5

Christ followers: Galatians 3:16

OBSCURE
Bible Facts

Tekoa, where Amos was a shepherd, was 11 miles south of Jerusalem. The Desert of Tekoa was also the place where Jehoshaphat set out with his army led by singers (2 Chronicles 20:20).

DAY FOUR: REFLECT
So What?

Today I want you to spend time simply thinking about how all the information in this week's study relates to you. Consider it a So What? day. Here are a few questions to ponder. Feel free to camp out on only one if that is where the Holy Spirit leads you.

1. God called Amos to a difficult task. Although Amos's resume didn't seem to coincide with the job description, Amos obeyed God. Is God calling you to a difficult task? Do you feel you lack qualifications? Does that matter to God? How should you respond?

2. Amos prophesied during a wealthy and prosperous time. What attitudes develop during times of prosperity? Have you ever experienced these? Do you believe our country has experienced them? Why or why not?

3. The rampant injustice in Israel during Amos's day displeased God. What kinds of injustices do you see in our world today? How should you respond? Why?

4. Religion held a prominent position during this time, as it does in our society. What similarities do you see in the practice of religion in our culture and that of ancient Israel's? Are you guilty of any of the same rituals? If so, what are they?

5. God pronounced a horrible judgment on Israel, yet he did not leave his people without hope. In one of the last verses of the book of Amos, God says of a later time: "I will bring back my exiled people Israel; they will rebuild the ruined cities and live in them. . . . I will plant Israel in their own land, never again to be uprooted from the land I have given them" (Amos 9:14, 15). What does this teach you about God? Why is this important in your life today?

Holy Preservation

Amos declared God's message with a roar and made sure the people knew that the Lion himself was speaking. Lives lived so unashamedly against God and his ways could not be overlooked. Devastating judgment was coming—in the form of Assyria in 722 BC. God foretold this through his messenger Amos, and the picture was not pretty:

. . . .

An enemy will overrun the land; he will pull down your strongholds and plunder your fortresses. (3:11)

As a shepherd saves from the lion's mouth only two leg bones or a piece of an ear, so will the Israelites be saved. (3:12)

I will tear down the winter house along with the summer house; the houses adorned with ivory will be destroyed and the mansions will be demolished. (3:15)

The city that marches out a thousand strong for Israel will have only a hundred left; the town that marches out a hundred strong will have only ten left. (5:3)

There will be wailing in all the streets and cries of anguish in every public square. The farmers will be summoned to weep and the mourners to wail. There will be wailing in all the vineyards. (5:16, 17)

I will send you into exile beyond Damascus. (5:27)

For the LORD God Almighty declares, "I will stir up a nation against you, O house of Israel, that will oppress you all the way from Lebo Hamath to the valley of the Arabah." (Amos 6:14)

. . . .

You see, a holy God cannot tolerate sin because sin opposes holiness. A. W. Tozer, in his book *The Knowledge of the Holy*, describes God's intolerance like this: "Since God's first concern for His universe is its moral health, that is, its holiness, whatever is contrary to this is necessarily under His eternal displeasure. To preserve His creation God must destroy whatever would destroy it. When He arises to put down iniquity and save the world from irreparable moral collapse, He is said to be angry. Every wrathful judgment in the history of the world has been a holy act of preservation. The holiness of God, the wrath of God, and the health of the creation are inseparably united. God's wrath is His utter intolerance of whatever degrades and destroys."[35]

A just God cannot let sin go unpunished. Yet by punishing the wrongdoer, God is truly working to draw people to himself. It is a picture of his love for us. In *God: As He Longs for You to See Him*, author Chip Ingram suggests, "God loves us so much that when we choose to step outside of the boundaries of his holiness, certain consequences act like a vise to bring judgment into our lives to correct us until we say, 'I yield.'"[36] It makes sense then to hear Amos declare, "Let justice roll on like a river" (5:24), for when God's justice rolls, his love for his people is displayed.

And God loved Israel, his chosen nation, his firstborn son (Exodus 4:22). Moses wrote in Deuteronomy that the Lord declared Israel to be "his people, his treasured possession" (26:18). God also declared that he would set Israel's "praise, fame and honor high above all the nations he has made and that [Israel] will be a people holy to the LORD" (v. 19). Isaiah recorded God's thoughts toward his people by saying, "I [God] have redeemed you; I have summoned you by name; you are mine. . . . You are precious and honored in my sight, and . . . I love you" (Isaiah 43:1, 4). Jeremiah proclaimed God's heart toward Israel when he wrote, "I [God] have loved you with an everlasting love; I have drawn you with loving-kindness" (Jeremiah 31:3).

God's justice is a by-product of his love.

Riding in tandem with justice is righteousness. Amos said, "Let justice roll on like a river, righteousness like a never-failing stream!" (5:24).

When a body produces cancerous cells, those cells need to be cut out so the healthy ones can thrive. Similarly, God's justice guarantees an environment where righteousness can flourish. God's goal for Israel was the emergence of righteousness. Through Israel all the nations of the earth would be blessed (Genesis 12:1-3), so God had to ensure that Israel remained healthy. Pure. Righteous.

In the movie *A Knight's Tale,* Heath Ledger's character, William Thatcher, enlists the help of his ragtag, colorful comrades to write a letter to his love, Jocelyn. Each member of the hodgepodge group adds his two-cents' worth with the closing offered by their female blacksmith. She insists the letter be signed with hope. "Love," she says, "should end with hope."[37]

The message of Amos does just that. It ends with hope. After calling the Israelites out for their blatant disregard of God's ways and delivering the news of the nation's imminent destruction, Amos ends with a word of optimistic expectation. After all is said and done, after God's judgment is delivered, after the punishment is doled out, God would make good on a promise. A promise to rebuild the ruined city. A promise to return the exiles to their land. A promise brought about by love. Because "love should end with hope."

DAY FIVE: REMEMBER
A God Who Restores

Comfortable Christianity. It's an oxymoron, like jumbo shrimp, replete with contradiction. Amos, the small-town, Judean, everyman prophet understood contradiction and called the Israelites on the carpet for their ritualistic righteousness. Like the Israelites, we get comfortable in our religiosity and need a wake-up call. Amos shows us that, by assessing our comfortable situation and confessing our pet sins, we can cling to the hope of God's promise of restoration!

1. Pick a verse to memorize. Write it out and say it over and over and over throughout the week.

2. Continue to add to your "Things I've Learned About God" list or chart. There is much to glean about God in this week's lesson.

The Call's for You

Whew! What a message. What a task. I'm sure this fig farmer felt out of his league, yet he faithfully did what God asked him to do. What about you? How is God asking you to step out of your comfort zone? Are you feeling a little unqualified? Not a problem! God has a tendency to use the unqualified, so we all should feel right at home! Consider these folks:

- Kim, a nurse who installs plumbing systems so Haitian families can receive clean water.

- Steve and Craig, paint makers who plant churches. Their goal: to bring as many people with them to heaven as is *in*humanly possible!

- Lori, a minister without a degree who effectively counsels and encourages church ministry staff.

- Pat, a retired teacher with a heart for missions. She travels worldwide encouraging missionaries in their calling for the kingdom.

- LeAnne, a stay-at-home mom who writes Bible studies so people can know God by knowing his word.

Whatever task God is calling you to, rest in the fact that you are unqualified.

What? Did you read that correctly? Yup. Because it's not about our qualifications, it's about our God. With him nothing is impossible (Luke 1:37), and in our weakness he is our strength (2 Corinthians 12:9, 10).

So embrace the task. Step out in confidence—knowing that the God of the universe has called you. And it would behoove you to answer that call!

OBSCURE OBSERVATIONS

CHAPTER EIGHT

Be careful that the urgent doesn't crowd out the important.
—Unknown

haggai and zechariah:
prophets with a purpose

SETTING PRIORITIES • HAGGAI 1, 2; ZECHARIAH 4

Spiritual ADD

"Look in my eyes!" I said frequently when trying to impart direction or correction to my young son. His eyes wandered and he missed the message I was diligently trying to relay. I'd have to take his little face in my hands and hold his head still while reiterating the words he couldn't seem to hear. A bird flying past the window, a commercial popping up on TV, or even the buzz of the clothes dryer shifted his focus from the matter at hand. And once again I'd say, "Honey, look in Mommy's eyes!"

Understanding came in the third grade. After extensive testing and interviewing by a myriad of experts, my eight-year-old son was found to have attention deficit disorder (ADD).

Israel suffered from ADD of a spiritual nature. God had declared judgment on Israel and Judah because of the people's idolatry and absolute disregard for his commands. This judgment began when Assyria conquered Israel in 722 BC. Babylon invaded Judah three times and completed God's judgment on Judah in 586 BC when the temple in Jerusalem was destroyed and the Babylonians carried the Jews into captivity. Years later, when the Babylonian empire fell to the Medes and the Persians, the new ruler, Cyrus, reversed the Babylonian policy of resettlement and allowed the Jewish exiles to return to their homeland. Knowing that God's temple, his house, lay in ruins, a small remnant of Jews headed to Jerusalem to rebuild the sacred dwelling.

Led by their governor, Zerubbabel, and the high priest, Joshua, the people began the work about 536 BC. But distractions and problems with focus prevented the group from finishing the task until two prophets, Haggai and Zechariah, took Israel's face in their hands and said, "Look in our eyes! We have a message for you!" And what a message it was, for it was from God himself!

········•●•········

DAY ONE: READ
Refocus

The first group of Jews headed back to Jerusalem in 536 BC. This Jewish remnant living in Jerusalem received God's message from Haggai in 520 BC, during the reign of another Persian king, Darius.

1. Understanding that background, read the following passages and write out a synopsis of the historical happenings:

   Ezra 1:1-4

Ezra 3:8

Ezra 4:4, 24

Ezra 5:1, 2

Ezra 6:14, 15

232 obscure no more

2. Haggai is a short book, only two chapters. Take time to read and reread
   these two chapters. If possible, read through it in at least two different
   versions. Answer the following questions based on your reading:

Who was Haggai?

What was the main problem he was confronting?

God gives Haggai four different messages to deliver to the Israelites.
Each is identified by the calendar day that Haggai received it. Complete the chart for each of the four messages.

When was the message delivered?	What problem was confronted?	List some indicators of this problem.	What was God's main message?
Second year of Darius; first day of the sixth month			Give careful thought to _____ (Haggai 1:5, 7).
	Making comparisons		Be _____ (Haggai 2:4). I will fill _____ (Haggai 2:7).
			From this day on I will _____ (Haggai 2:19).
	n/a	n/a	(Regarding Zerubbabel) I have _____ (Haggai 2:23).

How did the leaders and/or the people respond to Haggai's messages? When did they respond?

Over what or whom does God have power? List answers below with the appropriate Scripture references.

Consider Your Ways!

Have you ever gotten your priorities out of whack? A good book can thwart my best intentions regarding priorities. When I'm engrossed in the pages of one of my favorite authors, everything else seems to be neglected. Dental appointment? I guess that will have to wait another six months! Dinner? Peanut butter is in the pantry. Laundry? Pick something out of the dirty-clothes bin and shake it a few times; it will be fine. Children? Oh! Was I supposed to pick them up from school?

Priorities usually go deeper than that, though, don't they? We're talking about valuing God, people, and things in such a way that our life and lifestyle are directly impacted.

We say we love God with all our heart, mind, soul, and strength, but do we really? We say we love others as ourselves, but do we really? We say we hold loosely to the things in our lives, but do we really?

I've seen examples of those who got it . . . I mean really got it. They truly understood what was important in life. One couple in particular comes to mind. I only spent one week of my life with them and can only remember their first names, but Rod and Sandy's lives and lifestyle I will never forget. Business owners in Ohio who were nearing retirement, they would have had a very comfortable and wonderful retirement had they stayed in Ohio because their family, including beloved children and grandchildren, lived nearby. But Rod and Sandy felt led to move to the Dominican Republic to be the host and hostess of a Christian mission there. They sold everything they had accumulated in life, went to school to learn Spanish, and headed to a small town on a rugged island thousands of miles from family and friends.

Serving mission groups as they came from the States was their assigned task. They cooked for, cleaned up after, and ministered to the needs of benevolent strangers on short-term mission trips. The short-termers were then free to focus on the tasks at hand.

Loving God. Loving people. Holding things loosely.

I've also seen those who didn't get it. Their focus was off. Priorities got blurred, and God and their loved ones were put on the back burner, pushed aside for something far less significant.

The Israelites fell into this latter category. God had witnessed a shift in their focus and was not pleased. Initially, the people were committed to rebuilding God's house. But when times got tough and discouragement set in, they decided to focus on their own homes instead. And God had something to say about that! "Now this is what the LORD Almighty says: 'Give careful thought to your ways. You have planted much, but have harvested little. You eat, but never have enough. You drink, but never have your fill. You put on the clothes, but are not warm. You earn wages, only to put them in a purse with holes in it'" (Haggai 1:5, 6). For sixteen years, God said, the people of Israel had been hopelessly unproductive: "You expected much, but see, it turned out to be little. What you brought home, I blew away. Why? . . . Because of my house, which remains a ruin, while each of you is busy with his own house" (v. 9).

Through Haggai, God called the Israelites to think carefully and consider their ways! What about us? What do we focus on? Are we more concerned about the state and status of our own "kingdoms" than God's kingdom? Have our priorities shifted in such a way that the outcome of our efforts is merely making us work harder? Where does God fit into our list of priorities? If we have sensed a shift in our priorities, maybe it's time to consider God's message and take it to heart. "Consider your ways!" (v. 7, *NASB*).

Ouch! Hits a nerve, doesn't it? Sometimes being confronted with an ugly truth hurts, yet that hurt can produce positive changes. Surprisingly, Israel responded in a positive way. When confronted with the truth, the people obeyed the voice of the Lord and showed reverence to him (v. 12). God reassured them that he was the strength behind their efforts (v. 13; Zechariah 4:6), and then he stirred up their spirits and they began (again) their work on the house of the Lord (Haggai 1:14).

What work needs to be begun again in your life? Consider your ways . . . obey God's voice . . . and you can know God will empower you and stir your spirit too.

DAY TWO: READ
By My Spirit

Zechariah was another prophet used by God to help the Israelites keep their focus. While Haggai got the people moving again on the temple-building project, Zechariah encouraged them to finish their work. Through a series of eight visions, God gave Zechariah his message. Zechariah 4 records the fifth vision and specifically targets Israel's leaders.

Then the angel who had been talking with me returned and woke me, as though I had been asleep. "What do you see now?" he asked.

I answered, "I see a solid gold lampstand with a bowl of oil on top of it. Around the bowl are seven lamps, each one having seven spouts with wicks. And I see two olive trees, one on each side of the bowl." Then I asked the angel, "What are these, my lord? What do they mean?"

"Don't you know?" the angel asked.

"No, my lord," I replied.

Then he said to me, "This is what the Lord says to Zerubbabel: It is not by force nor by strength, but by my Spirit, says the Lord of Heaven's Armies. Nothing, not even a mighty mountain, will stand in Zerubbabel's way; it will become a level plain before him! And when Zerubbabel sets the final stone of the Temple in place, and the people will shout: 'May God bless it! May God bless it!'"

Then another message came to me from the Lord: "Zerubbabel is the one who laid the foundation of this Temple, and he will complete it. Then you will know that the Lord of Heaven's Armies has sent me. Do not despise these small beginnings, for the Lord rejoices to see the work begin, to see the plumb line in Zerubbabel's hand."

(The seven lamps represent the eyes of the Lord that search all around the world.)

Then I asked the angel, "What are these two olive trees on each side of the lampstand, and what are the two olive branches that pour out golden oil through two gold tubes?"

"Don't you know?" he asked.

"No, my lord," I replied.

Then he said to me, "They represent the two heavenly beings who stand in the court of the Lord of all the earth." (Zechariah 4, *NLT*)

. . . .

1. Answer the following questions from the text:

What was on top of the solid gold lampstand?

What was on each side of the bowl?

According to the angel, what message was being given to Zerubbabel?

By way of review (Haggai 1:1), who was Zerubbabel?

What would stand in Zerubbabel's way?

What would Zerubbabel do?

What was not to be despised?

What do the seven lamps represent?

What do the two olive trees represent?

2. Sometimes Old Testament visions can be difficult to understand. Let's look closer at a few parts of this message to make certain we grasp its intent.

The lampstand (Isaiah 60:1-3; 62:1)

Who is the lampstand?

What is the lampstand's purpose?

The oil (Exodus 30:22-33; Luke 4:14-20; Acts 1:8)

How was oil used?

Who had anointed Jesus?

From where does our power come?

The olive trees (Haggai 1:1; 2:2)

Who were the two men called to lead the rebuilding of the temple in Jerusalem?

3. Why would these words be an encouragement to Zerubbabel?

4. How can these words be an encouragement to you?

Consider Your God!

Comparisons. We all make them—about appearances, economic status, education, relationships, talents or abilities, and more. Danger lurks in making comparisons, because Satan uses them to keep us from being effective and productive. We think we're not good enough, smart enough, or talented enough to step up and do the task God has called us to. We buy into the devil's lie that we're not as qualified as the next guy, that we are somehow less than what God needs. Rather than walking in faith, we talk ourselves out of taking the first step. The task is never attempted, let alone accomplished!

God Is with Us

The people of Israel just about talked themselves out of completing the temple by making a comparison. Those who had seen the first temple realized that the new one would not be able to match the splendor of Solomon's temple (Ezra 3:12; Haggai 2:3). But God shifted their focus from the temple's shell to the one who filled it with his glory: "'I will shake all nations, and the desired of all nations will come, and I will fill this house with glory,' says the LORD Almighty. 'The silver is mine and the gold is mine,' declares the LORD Almighty. 'The glory of this present house will be greater than the glory of the former house,' says the LORD Almighty. 'And in this place I will grant peace,' declares the LORD Almighty" (Haggai 2:7-9).

Did you notice the number of times God's name is used in this short passage? Four times we read "the LORD Almighty." And in this two-chapter book, "the LORD Almighty" is mentioned a total of fourteen times! By using this name, God is declaring that he is Lord of all! As a matter of fact, other translations read "Lord of hosts" or "Lord of Heaven's Armies," which aptly describe God's rule and reign, for he is Lord of the heavenly hosts, he is Lord of the earth, he is Lord of the sun, moon, and stars. He is Lord of all creation! When he declares something, we ought to trust that it will happen!

It makes me wonder if God sits in amazement at the smallness of our thinking. Is he saying to us, "You've got to be kidding?" when we begin questioning and comparing? His desire is for us to consider him—his power, his riches, his glory, and his purpose. When we do, any daunting assignment suddenly diminishes considerably. And when we consider that he is with us, it gives us the strength we need to work. "'Be strong, all you people of the land,' declares the LORD, 'and work. For I am with you,' declares the LORD Almighty" (Haggai 2:4).

God Is in Us

Not only does this understanding of God *with* us apply to the tasks God has called us to, but we can also learn something by regarding who we are *in* him. So often when comparisons enter our minds, we begin to feel inadequate and unworthy. Our self-esteem wanes. We experience a sort of paralysis and are unable to take the necessary steps toward obedience. Have you ever experienced this? I have, on many occasions.

One such occasion came when my husband was praying through a decision regarding a short-term mission trip. He had specifically been sought out to go with a group from the Boston area. The team needed a doctor to head up the medical side of things. Since Ron's heart for missions beats strong and he had the qualifications, the decision was a relative no-brainer. Once he determined his involvement, he asked me to pray about going.

"Me?" I said. "I'm not medical! I can't even look at my kids' sore throats without gagging."

Ron's response: "Just pray about it. *Then* make your decision."

Determined to make my case to God, my prayers were very one-sided. I couldn't possibly go because I had nothing to offer. I shared my inadequacies with God and then said, "Amen." For a while my ears (and heart) stayed closed to what God had to say. But shortly after these one-sided conversations began, I attended a women's conference at our church. As I waited for a workshop to begin, an older lady sat down beside me and introduced herself. Immediately I recognized her name, for she was a missionary who had recently returned to the States after serving a lifetime in Africa.

Effie Giles, I found out, was a warm, wonderful servant of God.

We ended up having lunch together that day. I asked her questions about the work she and her husband had done and sat mesmerized by her simple yet powerful stories. At the end of our time together, I told her I was praying through a decision to go on a mission trip but felt I didn't have a whole lot to offer. "All the others have specific roles or tasks," I said. "They have specialized training. I'm a stay-at home mom."

"Oh, honey!" Effie replied. "You are a vital part of the body of Christ, and you have his Spirit in you! That makes you more than qualified. And I'll tell you something else, those missionaries need encouragement, and you're the one to do that."

Long story short, I went. I met Rod and Sandy. And while everyone else went off to build the school and treat the patients, I hung out with our hosts. We went to the market together. We shopped together. We worked in the kitchen together. We cleaned up together. All the while, Rod and Sandy shared the story of their transition from Ohio to the Dominican Republic and some of the struggles associated with it. I listened. And each night I returned to my room to entreat God to encourage these sweet saints.

As the week progressed, Rod and I came up with a project that had been neglected and overlooked by other groups, and the requirements for the job suited my talents perfectly—cleaning and painting, two things I am really good at, if I do say so myself! The school's bathrooms were in need of a major overhaul, so I recruited two other ladies who were feeling a bit underutilized to work with me. Together we accomplished much. It was extraordinary!

I'm thankful Effie took my face in her hands, so to speak, and reminded me that God is in me. Imagine her doing the same for you. Because you are glorious! If you are a Christ follower, God resides in you. You are the temple; he is the resident. "Do you not know that your body is a temple of the Holy Spirit, who is in you, whom you have received from God?" (1 Corinthians 6:19). He's saying, "Because I am in you, you can know that there are no comparisons! You are glorious!"

What an amazing concept to cling to. What an amazing truth to embrace.

And with this truth in tow, the Israelites got a move on and finished the work.

With this truth in tow, why don't we do the same!

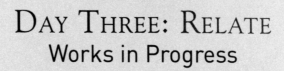

Day Three: Relate
Works in Progress

1. I want us to look at a few role models from Scripture. The Israelites had been given the assignment to rebuild the house of the Lord, and like them, the following individuals were all given divine assignments as well. Look up the passages, seeking to find their divine assignments and their attitudes toward their work.

   Paul

   Assignment (Galatians 1:15, 16):

   Attitude (Philippians 1:21):

   John the Baptist

   Assignment (John 3:28):

Attitude (John 3:30):

Peter

Assignment (John 21:15-17):

Attitude (1 Peter 5:1, 2):

Mary

Assignment (Luke 1:26-33):

Attitude (Luke 1:38):

2. Look up the following verses and write out a summary of each:

Matthew 6:33

2 Chronicles 16:9 (first sentence)

Galatians 2:20

Hebrews 12:1, 2

3. What is the common thread you find woven throughout the lives of those in question 1 and the passages in question 2?

We read about these giants in Scripture and the directives of how we are to live. Maybe you are inspired. If so, great! Maybe you're overwhelmed and discouraged. If so, hang in there! Philippians 1:6 says, "He who began a good work in you will carry it on to completion." *The Message* says it like this: "There has never been the slightest doubt in my mind that the God who started this great work in you would keep at it and bring it to a flourishing finish on the very day Christ Jesus appears." So rest in the fact that we are all works in progress and that the Lord Almighty himself is the one working in us and through us!

Consider Your Efforts!

"You're on a three-month probation. I'll be watching you." Most employees hear these words when first hired. During that time frame, employers look to see whether the new employee will perform the job with wholehearted effort and sincere diligence. If yes, the new hire stays on. Rewards follow. If not . . . well, let's just say the employee might need to brush up on interview skills, among other things!

Three months to the day after the Israelites restarted work on the temple, God gave another message through Haggai: "From this day on I will bless you" (Haggai 2:19). We've already seen that when the Israelites focused on themselves, their hard work resulted in little return; God refused to bless when the people refused to obey. Their disobedience and halfhearted efforts would not be tolerated. God wanted his people to understand the connection: "'So it is with this people and this nation in my sight,' declares the LORD. 'Whatever they do and whatever they offer there is defiled. Now give careful thought to this from this day on—consider how things were before one stone was laid on another in the LORD's temple. When anyone came to a heap of twenty measures, there were only ten. When anyone went to a wine vat to draw fifty measures, there were only twenty'" (vv. 14-16).

You would think the Israelites would have picked up on the connection between disobedience (defilement) and the lack of blessing, but they were a bit thickheaded. God urgently wanted to get Israel's attention, so he resorted to other methods: "'I struck all the work of your hands with blight, mildew and hail, yet you did not turn to me,' declares the LORD" (v. 17).

Still the Israelites did not understand. Their efforts were being thwarted by God Almighty because they were operating with unclean, half-motivated hearts. That's when God called in his prophets. Haggai and Zechariah had to take hold of Israel's face and force the people to hear God's message. The Israelites said they got it, but God had them in a probationary period of sorts as he waited for the proof. Within those few months, they proved their efforts were sincere and their ways had changed. This repentant attitude and wholehearted devotion brought about God's blessing: "From this day on I will bless you" (v. 19).

Is there a connection between our efforts and attitudes in serving God and the blessings (or lack of them) that result? Consider these verses:

· ·

But seek first his kingdom and his righteousness, and all these things will be given to you as well. (Matthew 6:33)

And without faith it is impossible to please God, because anyone who comes to him must believe that he exists and that he rewards those who earnestly seek him. (Hebrews11:6)

· ·

There is a definite principle at play here, and a definite message: our efforts in combination with our attitude and our audience will determine our outcome. Please understand that I'm not preaching a health-and-wealth gospel. We know that in this world we will have trouble (John 16:33). But when you are earnestly seeking to serve the one who overcomes the world, you can be guaranteed a blessing—a reward—given by the giver of every good and perfect gift (James 1:17).

Whom are you seeking to serve? Is your service wholehearted and faith based, or is it lacking luster and grounded in the flesh? Consider your efforts! And consider the one toward whom they are directed. God probably won't have you in a three-month probationary period, but you can be assured he will be watching . . . and waiting to reward with blessings. "For the eyes of the LORD range throughout the earth to strengthen those whose hearts are fully committed to him" (2 Chronicles 16:9).

OBSCURE
Bible Facts

Talk about a hard night! Zechariah experienced all eight visions he had during the course of one night. They were not dreams, for the prophet was fully awake (1:8).

DAY FOUR: REFLECT
Assessment

There have been many times in my life when I've lost focus and my priorities have gone askew. Maybe you can relate. In our minds we rank our priorities a certain way, but if we truly evaluated things, what would our evaluation reveal? Let's find out.

1. List your top five priorities in order of importance: greatest to least.

2. Ask a significant person in your life (your spouse, child, friend, roommate, etc.) to list the top few priorities he or she sees you living out. (To get an even broader perspective, ask several people for their input.) Summarize what you learn.

3. Think through your schedule from the past week. If you can, quantify the number of hours you spent on each of those priorities. Write that number next to the list in question 1. If there were other things on which you spent a bulk of time, write those down and the number of hours associated with each.

4. Reflect on your findings. Did they reveal what you thought they would? Why or why not?

5. Look up Matthew 22:37-39. Write out the verses.

6. Think back on the main messages Haggai and Zechariah gave to the Israelites and their leaders. Can these relate to you? If so, how?

My goal today is not to lay a guilt trip on anyone but rather to help you assess your focus and seek God's direction to make changes wherever necessary. So spend some time in prayer right now. Ask God to open your eyes to your true priorities. Seek his wisdom and his power to make adjustments in:

- Your schedule

- Your lifestyle

- Your relationships

- _____ (fill in the blank)

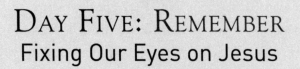

DAY FIVE: REMEMBER
Fixing Our Eyes on Jesus

1. What verse spoke to your heart this week? Maybe it was one that con-victed you. Maybe it was one that encouraged you. Write it out. Memo-rize it. Say it aloud to a friend or family member. Review the verses you have memorized from previous lessons as well.

2. We learned much about God and his character this week. Add what you learned to your list or chart, referencing the appropriate Bible verses.

Consider Your Task!

Remember the awful and often life-scarring tradition of choosing teams on the playground? Two captains alternated picking players until only the few undesirables remained. Those few left behind knew they were not the most qualified and were therefore not wanted.

It's every kid's dream to be picked, to be chosen. Let's face it, it's every adult's dream too. Thankfully, our heavenly Father understands this.

Sixteen years had come and gone, and the temple still was not completed. Zerubbabel, the leader of this project, certainly must have felt like a failure. He could not keep his task force focused on the vision. They got distracted, and the work ceased completely. God's messengers got hold of the people of Israel and ignited the fire for them to get back to work. But what about their leader? God knew a special message needed to be given to Zerubbabel, and so he gave it, in dual form.

Zechariah said it like this: "This is the word of the Lord to Zerubbabel: 'Not by might nor by power, but by my Spirit,' says the Lord Almighty. . . . 'The hands of Zerubbabel have laid the foundation of this temple; his hands will also complete it'" (Zechariah 4:6, 9).

Haggai continued the motivational speech: "'On that day,' declares the Lord Almighty, 'I will take you, my servant Zerubbabel son of Shealtiel,' declares the Lord, 'and I will make you like my signet ring, for I have chosen you,' declares the Lord Almighty" (Haggai 2:23).

I can imagine Zerubbabel thinking, *Me? You have chosen me, God? But I'm the one who couldn't keep the people motivated! I'm the one who let the project fail!*

Then I imagine God responding, "No, Zerubbabel. You're the one I have chosen. I'm picking you to be a major player on my winning team. And together we will finish this project."

How encouraging!

And how encouraging for us too, because God has called each of us to hold a key position on his team. We know from the book of Acts that King David was placed in his generation to serve God's purpose (Acts 13:36). The same can be said of Esther and Joshua and Moses and Ruth and Paul and Peter and . . . *you*! You have been chosen. You have been picked. You are wanted and desired and are aided by God's Spirit to do a mighty work for God's kingdom. Yes, you! Go . . . and consider your task!

It's all about focus, isn't it? The Israelites got their priorities mixed up, but God used two prophets to get their attention and fix their eyes on the only one who can truly bring help and hope.

Oh—and just so you know, my eight-year-old ADD son is now a fully functioning, attentive adult. And the best thing: the cumbersome diagnosis given him in the third grade aided in a laser focus on the author and finisher of his faith, Jesus Christ (Hebrews 12:2, *KJV*).

Getting Started

1. Howard G. Hendricks and William D. Hendricks, *Living by the Book: The Art and Science of Reading the Bible*, rev. ed. (1991; Chicago: Moody Publishers, 2007), 77.

2. Ibid., 100.

3. Ibid., 131.

4. Kay Arthur, *How to Study Your Bible: The Lasting Rewards of the Inductive Approach* (Eugene, Oregon: Harvest House Publishers, 1994), 65.

Korah & Company

5. http://www.thatsweird.net/history6.shtml (accessed December 14, 2009).

6. A transcript of the August 8, 2008, interview can be found at www.abcnews.go.com/print?id=5544981 (accessed December 20, 2009).

7. The Barna Group, Ltd., "New Research Explores How Different Generations View and Use the Bible," October 19, 2009, http://www.barna.org/barna-update/article/12-faithspirituality/317-new-research-explores-how-different-generations-view-and-use-the-bible (accessed December 19, 2009).

8. The Barna Group, Ltd., "Americans Are Exploring New Ways of Experiencing God," June 8, 2009, http://www.barna.org/barna-update/article/12-faithspirituality/270-americans-are-exploring-new-ways-of-experiencing-god (accessed December 19, 2009).

9. Ted Olsen, "Buffy's Religion," *Christianity Today*, July 8, 2002, http://www.christianitytoday.com/ct/article_print.html?id=8652 (accessed December 20, 2009).

10. Vance Havner, quoted by Chuck Swindoll, ed., in *The Tale of the Tardy Oxcart* (Nashville: Word Publishing, 1998), 475.

Achan

11. Spiros Zodhiates, ed., *Hebrew-Greek Key Word Study Bible: Key Insights into God's Word* (Chattanooga: AMG Publishers, 2008), 1875.

12. http://www.blueletterbible.org/lang/lexicon/lexicon.cfm?Strongs=H2530&t=NIV (accessed December 1, 2009).

13. Bill Hybels, *Axiom* (Grand Rapids: Zondervan, 2008), 12.

Deborah and Jael

14. Charles Dickens opened *A Tale of Two Cities* (1859) with this now-famous line.

15. http://www.mediaed.org/Handouts/ChildrenMedia.pdf (accessed March 6, 2010).

16. http://www.johnstonsarchive.net/policy/abortion/graphusabrate.html (accessed February 17, 2008).

17. "The States of Our Unions," http://www.psychologytoday.com/articles/200001/the-states-our-unions (accessed March 3, 2010).

18. http://www.snopes.com/radiotv/tv/marykay.asp (accessed February 17, 2008).

19. Christopher Lyon, "The Frog, the Kettle and the Couch," *Focus on the Family* magazine, couples edition, March 2008, http://www2.focusonthefamily.com/focusmagazine/spiritualheritage/A000001072.cfm (accessed March 6, 2010).

20. "How to Raise Kids: Stay Home or Go to Work?" February 23, 2006, http://abcnews.go.com/print?id=1653069 (accessed February 17, 2008).

21. Linda R. Hirshman, "Unleashing the Wrath of Stay-at-Home Moms," *The Washington Post*, June 18, 2006, www.washingtonpost.com/wp-dyn/content/article/2006/06/16/AR2006061601766.html (accessed February 17, 2008).

22. Linda Hirshman, "Homeward Bound," *The American Prospect*, November 21, 2005, http://www.prospect.org/cs/articles?article=homeward_bound (accessed February 17, 2008).

23. http://unabridged.merriam-webster.com

24. Max Lucado, *God Came Near* (Portland, Oregon: Multnomah Press, 1987), 89.

Mephibosheth

25. Kay Arthur, *Our Covenant God* (Colorado Springs: WaterBrook Press, 1999), 97–98.

26. Ibid., 116–117.

27. http://www.blueletterbible.org/lang/lexicon/lexicon.cfm?Strongs=H3810&t=NASB (accessed December 10, 2009) and http://www.blueletterbible.org/lang/lexicon/lexicon.cfm?Strongs=H1699&t=KJV (accessed December 10, 2009).

Adonijah

28. In 2005 the American Film Institute published a list of 400 memorable movie quotes. With one exception, all of the movie quotes in this chapter are taken from that list, which can be found at http://connect.afi.com/site/DocServer/quotes400 .pdf?docID=205 (accessed 3/9/10). The film credits here are listed in the order of the appearance of their respective quotations in this chapter.
James Cameron, screenwriter, *Titanic* (Paramount/Twentieth Century Fox, 1997).

Noel Langley, Florence Ryerson, and Edgar Allan Woolf, screenwriters, *The Wizard of Oz* (MGM, 1939). Spoken by Margaret Hamilton as the Wicked Witch of the West.

Leigh Brackett and Lawrence Kasdan, screenwriters, *Star Wars V: The Empire Strikes Back* (Twentieth Century Fox, 1980). Spoken by James Earl Jones as the voice of Darth Vader, played by David Prowse.

George Lucas, screenwriter, *Star Wars IV: A New Hope* (Twentieth Century Fox, 1977). Tim Dirks, "Great Film Taglines," http://www.filmsite.org/taglines3.html (accessed 10/2/09).

William Broyles, Jr., and Al Reinert, screenwriters, *Apollo 13* (Universal, 1995).

Joseph Stinson, screenwriter, *Sudden Impact* (Warner Bros., 1983).

James Cameron and William Wisher, Jr., screenwriters, *Terminator 2: Judgment Day* (TriStar, 1991).

Tom Schulman, screenwriter, *Dead Poets Society* (Touchstone, 1989).

Eleanor Bergstein, screenwriter, *Dirty Dancing* (Artisan, 1987).

Eric Roth, screenwriter, *Forrest Gump* (Paramount, 1994).

Julius J. Epstein, Philip G. Epstein, and Howard Koch, screenwriters, *Casablanca* (Warner Bros., 1942).

Jim Cash and Jack Epps, Jr., screenwriters, *Top Gun* (Paramount, 1986).

29. http://www.songlyrics.com/beastie-boys/fight-for-your-right-lyrics/ (accessed 10/2/09).

Jehoshaphat

30. Oliver Sacks, "To See and Not See: A Neurologist's Notebook," *The New Yorker,* May 10, 1993, http://www.newyorker.com/archive/1993/05/10/1993_05_10_059_TNY _CARDS_000362590 (accessed August 23, 2006).

Amos

31. See the factsheet "Bonded Slavery" at http://www.ijm.org/ourwork/whatwedo (accessed 4-5-10).

32. *Worship—That Thing We Do.* DVD. Choice Resources, 2002.

33. http://en.allexperts.com/q/Ancient-Classical-History-2715/Ancient-Greek-Actors .htm (accessed November 7, 2009).

34. http://www.blueletterbible.org/lang/lexicon/lexicon.cfm?Strongs=G5273&t=NASB (accessed November 7, 2009).

35. A. W. Tozer, *The Knowledge of the Holy* (New York: HarperCollins, 1961), 106.

36. Chip Ingram, *God: As He Longs for You to See Him* (Grand Rapids: Baker Books, 2004), 113.

37. *A Knight's Tale,* Columbia Pictures, 2001.

All epigraphs, except where otherwise noted, are quoted from Roy B. Zuck, *The Speaker's Quote Book* (Grand Rapids: Kregel, 1997).

WHAT I'VE LEARNED ABOUT GOD
from Korah & Company

Scripture References to Remember:

Thoughts to Remember:

WHAT I'VE LEARNED ABOUT GOD
from Achan

Scripture References to Remember:

Thoughts to Remember:

WHAT I'VE LEARNED ABOUT GOD
from Deborah and Jael

Scripture References to Remember:

Thoughts to Remember:

WHAT I'VE LEARNED ABOUT GOD
from Mephibosheth

Scripture References to Remember:

Thoughts to Remember:

WHAT I'VE LEARNED ABOUT GOD
from Adonijah

Scripture References to Remember:

Thoughts to Remember:

WHAT I'VE LEARNED ABOUT GOD
from Jehoshaphat

Scripture References to Remember:

Thoughts to Remember:

WHAT I'VE LEARNED ABOUT GOD
from Amos

Scripture References to Remember:

Thoughts to Remember:

WHAT I'VE LEARNED ABOUT GOD
from Haggai and Zechariah

Scripture References to Remember:

Thoughts to Remember:

The following pages provide you with a helpful outline of suggestions and questions to use for the group study of each chapter. Each guide offers:

> **Read This First:** Quickly gives you the main point of the lesson and the story from which the study comes. Also offers extra reading suggestions.
>
> **Relate to It:** An opening time of conversation. Suggested time: 10 minutes.
>
> **Reflect on It:** A time for deeper discussion and engagement with the Scriptures. Suggested time: 30 minutes.
>
> **Remember It:** Closing the group session with accountability and prayer. Members have the chance to share what they've learned and express personal needs. Suggested time: 20 minutes.

KORAH & COMPANY: A REBELLIOUS BROOD
Numbers 16:1-40

Read This First

Learn how to diagnose the disease of rebellion and understand the remedy offered through the Word of God. The story of Korah is the basis for this study.

Relate to It

Ask the following questions. Be prepared to share a story from your own experiences.

1. What fads or trends have you participated in? (e.g., legwarmers, mall bangs, Rubik's Cube, etc.)
2. What do you think made that activity or item so desirable?

Reflect on It

Approach Korah's case using medical terminology. First, review the patient's information.

Patient History: Numbers 16:1-40

Name: Korah

Occupation: Levites—separated to do the service of the tabernacle of the Lord

Cohorts: Dathan and Abiram (sons of Eliab), On (the son of Peleth)

Chief Complaint: Korah & Company felt Moses and Aaron had exalted themselves above the entire congregation and that they (Korah & Company) were worthy of the same exaltation.

Symptoms

Use these questions to discuss the symptoms Korah & Company exhibit as found in Numbers 16:1-40. (See Day Three and Four of the study.)

1. Which symptoms are the most worrisome to you? Explain why.

2. Which ones are you more familiar with? Share your experiences.

3. Pride affects everyone. Talk about the quote from John Edwards on page 40. Discuss this quote with the class. Can we relate to what he says at all? Has pride ever altered your perspective? How?

4. Israel had a history of being contentious (look at pages 32-33 to review some of the complaints made by the Israelites). But this is not an attitude confined to historical record. Today, pride and contentiousness often masquerade as positive values of our society, such as individualism, personal rights, and so-called spirituality. Read the quote from Sarah Michelle Gellar on being a spiritual person (p. 43). How does this attitude reflect pride and contentiousness? What do you think explains the prevalence of this thinking in today's society?

Prognosis

Based on the symptoms of Korah & Company, Moses made a prognosis (Numbers 16:30). Discuss that prognosis.

5. Why do you think Moses suggested that God would do something "totally new" as a sign? Was he testing God or was he speaking from God? Explain the reasons for your answer.

6. What was the actual progression of the disease? In other words, what was the outcome (Numbers 16:31-35)? What outcomes of the disease of pride have you seen in your life or in the lives of others?

Treatment

Discuss the "prescriptions" suggested in Day Four of the study.

7. Did any of these Bible-based prescriptions stand out to you more than the others? If so, why?

8. How well do you think the prescriptions match the symptoms of the disease? What does it take to make these medicines work?

9. Have you ever made use of a particular medicine from the Bible to treat your symptoms? What verse or verses helped you deal with the sin in your life?

10. God's Word can provide us with some pretty strong medication. Talk about why we often tend to want to skip taking it. What are some possible side effects from this kind of medicine that people might fear?

Remember It

If your group is larger than six, break down into smaller groups (no more than five or six in one group). Then do the following:

1. Pair up so you can say your memory verses to one another. Explain why you chose that particular verse.
2. Ask the following questions of each other and discuss your answers. Do you have any symptoms of rebellion in your life? What specifically can you do to remedy that and keep the disease at bay? How can you hold each other accountable in these areas?
3. Take some time to pray together, asking for protection for each other from the disease of pride.

ACHAN: A MAN WITH A SECRET
Joshua 7

Read This First

Gain a deeper understanding of sin's lure, cure, and legacy by studying the story of Achan. Extra reading: To make sure you have the bigger picture (context) of this story, read Joshua 6-8.

Relate to It

Ask the following questions. Be prepared to share a story from your own experiences.

1. Have you ever played the children's game called Mouse Trap? (Have someone in the group describe the game: The basic premise is to build a contraption which sets off a chain reaction to capture your opponents' mice, or game pieces. It is a domino effect.)
2. Have you ever said or done anything that set off a chain reaction on other people? Explain.

Reflect on It

Reconstruct the story by having various members of your group share one segment at a time. To make it more fun, start by telling a brief beginning segment of the story yourself. Then toss a bean bag to someone else. That person will tell the next part and then toss the bean bag to someone else, and so forth. When the story has been completed, ask the following questions.

1. What was your initial reaction after reading this story? Why? Do you feel the same after completing the lesson? Why or why not?

Sin's Lure

Answer these questions about the lure of sin for Achan.

2. What did you learn through your word study about the meaning of the word *coveted*?
3. In Day Two of the study, you were asked to compare the actions of Eve and Achan. What similarities or differences did you find in their actions?
4. *Lust* is one translation of the Greek word *epithumia*, which means a desire, craving, longing for what is forbidden. Compare your own actions to those of Achan and of Eve: What are you allowing yourself to see? How do you avoid situations that represent known temptations for you? Or do you find yourself lingering and longing for these things? Have you ever tried to hide your behavior?

Sin's Cure

Discuss the story of Achan in relation to our story.

5. How do the measures that God took with Achan reflect what we need to do with sin in our lives? (Refer to Matthew 5:29, 30 and Galatians 5:9.)

6. In what ways does the story of Achan reflect the story of Jesus' sacrifice for us? In what ways does it differ? (Refer to 2 Corinthians 5:21 and other verses from Day Three of the study.)

Sin's Legacy

We know how Achan's family was affected by his actions. But sometimes it's harder to tell what effects sin brings, or how far those effects can spread.

7. Read Numbers 14:18 and Deuteronomy 7:9, 10. Discuss the ripple effect of sin and the ripple effect of righteousness on you, your family, and other people you know. Think of a time when you were aware of sin's legacy in someone's life. What scars did the sin leave behind? What effects have you seen righteousness bring to people?

8. What kind of legacy are you leaving? What things can you be doing on a regular basis to build up this legacy in a positive way?

Remember It

If your group is larger than six, break down into smaller groups (no more than five or six in one group). Then do the following:

1. Pair up so you can say your memory verses to one another. Explain why you chose that particular verse.

2. Discuss what you learned about God through this study. Did anything surprise you? comfort you? disturb you? confuse you? What is one thing you learned that you were able to relate to your own relationship with God or to your current circumstances?

3. Ask the following questions of each other and discuss your answers. Are there any areas in your life you are trying to cover up or hide? This may be difficult to reveal, but it is the first step to freedom from sin. How can you hold each other accountable in these areas?

4. Seek ways to encourage one another. Realize that we are all on a level playing field, "for all have sinned and fall short of the glory of God" (Romans 3:23). Understand, too, that "there is no condemnation for those who are in Christ Jesus" (Romans 8:1). Praise God!

5. Spend time sharing prayer needs. Pray for one another.

Deborah and Jael: A career-driven woman and a stay-at-home mom
Judges 4, 5

Read This First

Understand that our lives have purpose in God's kingdom through studying the actions of two strong women, Deborah and Jael.

Relate to It

Ask the following questions. Be prepared to share a story from your own experiences.

1. When you were a child, what dreams did you have for your life? Has your life turned out better than you imagined? harder than you imagined? How have you seen God working through your dreams or disappointments?

2. Who are some of your female role models or heroines? Why? What specifically do you admire about them?

Reflect on It

Deborah and Jael are two drastically different personalities with two drastically different callings, yet both were used in a mighty way by our mighty God. Review their stories.

Knowing Their Condition

God had promised the Israelites that he would be their God and they would be his people. But after Joshua died, another generation arose—one who did not know God nor what he had done for the nation of Israel (Judges 2:10).

1. Discuss the ways our society has changed in the last century. (See the section in this chapter entitled "Sin's Slippery Slope.") Would you consider the current generation as one who does not know God? Why or why not?

2. Discuss your own comfort level with certain kinds of sin. Have you ever felt that you have become desensitized to sin in your life or in the lives of others? How can your reaction to sin in your life be part of your purpose?

Knowing Their Calling

Both Deborah and Jael were married women, but their lives included much more than the usual wifely duties.

3. What do you think about the life of Deborah? Lappidoth was her husband, and therefore would have been seen as the head of her household. Yet Deborah was, in some ways at least, leading the nation. What challenges do you think such a situation might have? What benefits might come from a woman being in this position?

4. Of course, it would have been hard for anyone to dispute the career path that Deborah took. The position of prophetess is a God-appointed one, not one she sought out on her own. Think about your own field of work or that of a woman you know. What part did God play in the obtaining of that job or career?

5. A word study of Jael's name reveals that the root of her name in Hebrew means "valuable, useful." In what ways did she live up to her name? In what ways was she valuable or useful?

6. Jael was living out her life as a wife and mother. We don't know whether this life was one she chose or one that was placed upon her. However, we do know that the situation of Sisera coming to her tent was one that was thrust upon her. She had several choices of what to do with that situation. List some of her possible options.

7. There are many times in our lives when we have situations thrust upon us. Take some time to share some examples of these times with each other. How does what we do in such times reveal what we believe about God?

Knowing Their God

Deborah and Jael were strong because they relied on a strong God.

8. Talk about the characteristics of God that are seen in this story: compassionate, omniscient, powerful, and surprising. Which one of these is most important to you? Which ones are evident in your relationship with God?

Remember It

If your group is larger than six, break down into smaller groups (no more than five or six in one group). Then do the following:

1. Pair up so you can say your memory verses to one another. Explain why you chose that particular verse.

2. Discuss what you learned about God through this study. Then spend some time sharing prayer needs. Pray that God will show you how to "arise" for his cause.

MEPHIBOSHETH: AN OVERLOOKED OUTCAST
2 Samuel 9

Read This First

Through the study of the story of Mephibosheth, we can gain a better understanding of the promises we have because of our covenant-keeping God. To establish the context of God's covenant, you may want to read: Genesis 12:1-3; 15; 17.

Relate to It

Ask the following questions. Be prepared to share a story from your own experiences.

1. Have you ever entered into a bad contract? What happened? Did you back out or follow through? Describe your experience.

Reflect on It

Make sure you and your group have studied/researched the concept of *covenant*. A great resource is the book *Our Covenant God* by Kay Arthur (Colorado Springs: WaterBrook Press, 1999.)

1. Talk about the seriousness of the kind of covenant made between David and Jonathan, as discussed in Day One of the study and in "Comrades and Covenants." What qualities of that kind of covenant appeal to you?

2. Do we make any covenants like this in modern-day life? List some examples and talk about how they are similar to or different from the biblical covenants we have looked at.

3. What did you learn from reading about the covenant between God and Abraham (Genesis 17)?

4. Do you believe that God has made a covenant with you? Why or why not? If so, how does this covenant affect your daily living?

5. Think about the actions of King David toward Mephibosheth. List the actions together. How are each of the actions opposite to what had been done to Mephibosheth in the past?

6. Read Ephesians 1:3-14 together. Have class members share stories that illustrate or define the following aspects of our inheritance:

   ● blessed (v. 3)

   ● chosen (v. 4)

   ● adopted (v. 5)

- redeemed (v. 7)
- forgiven (v. 7)
- given knowledge (v. 9)
- sealed (v. 13)
- guaranteed (v. 14)

7. What aspects of Mephibosheth's story are most interesting to you? What aspects of his story reflect our relationship with God?

Remember It

If your group is larger than six, break down into smaller groups (no more than five or six in one group). Then do the following:

1. Pair up so you can say your memory verses to one another. Explain why you chose that particular verse.

2. Discuss what you learned about God through this study. Then spend some time sharing prayer needs. Pray about ways the knowledge of God's promises can make a difference in our daily lives.

ADONIJAH: A WANNABE KING
1 Kings 1

Read This First

Through the study of Adonijah's story, realize the limits of our rights and the unlimited sovereignty of God. You may want to read 1 Kings 2 for context.

Relate to It

Ask the following questions. Be prepared to share a story from your own experiences.

1. Think of some movie characters who have fought for their rights. Which ones come to mind?

2. Have you ever felt you had the "right" to buy something or some service? What was it? Looking back on it now, do you think you deserved it? Why or why not?

Reflect on It

Adonijah not only wanted to play the starring role in this drama, he wanted to direct as well. But God had a different plot in mind.

1. List as many of the actions Adonijah took as you can remember (from 1 Kings 1). What did his actions reveal about what he thought of himself?

2. What did his actions reveal about what he thought about his father? the people he asked to support him? about the God of Israel?

3. Have you ever wanted to take charge of a position that didn't belong to you? Share that desire with the group. What did you do about it?

4. Is there anything wrong with being ambitious? What does it look like to have ambition and still be under God's sovereign will?

5. Who else in this story showed ambition? Who else wanted to direct the king? Were their actions suspect in any way? Why or why not?

6. Read over the passages from Day Three of the study. What did you learn from looking at what God does or gives in these verses? (Let each person share something they found interesting or intriguing about the character of God.)

7. From Day Four of the study, talk about one thing each person learned about one of the following subjects:
   - Parenting
   - Relationships
   - God's plans

- Wisdom
- Forgiveness
- Keeping your word
- Holding grudges
- Confronting sin
- Betrayal
- Manipulating circumstances
- Another subject

8. Finish this sentence with words you have heard people use in this context: I've got a right to _____. After sharing some ways to finish that sentence, talk about which "rights" we actually have.

9. Having a right to something implies you have ownership of something that entitles you to certain claims. Talent, hard work, dedication, birth order, tradition, wisdom, societal law, possession, or wealth—Which of these secures our rights to anything? As children of God, what do we have ownership of? Explain your answers.

Remember It

If your group is larger than six, break down into smaller groups (no more than five or six in one group). Then do the following:

1. Pair up so you can say your memory verses to one another. Explain why you chose that particular verse.

2. If time allows, have the whole group read through Philippians 2:1-11 together. Discuss in what ways these verses relate to the rights that we do or do not have.

3. Discuss what you learned about God through this study. Then spend some time sharing prayer needs. Pray for one another.

JEHOSHAPHAT: A GOD-SEEKING LEADER
2 Chronicles 20

Read This First

Understand and assimilate Jehoshaphat's battle plan for dealing with fear as found in 2 Chronicles 20:1-30.

Relate to It

Ask the following questions. Be prepared to share a story from your own experiences.

1. Share a fear you had when you were a child. Where did that fear come from?
2. What comforted you when you were young? Who did you rely on to calm your fears?

Reflect on It

Three great nations had come together to make war against Judah. Let's look at Jehoshaphat's emotional and strategic response.

1. Jehoshaphat was told a vast army is coming. How was his initial response different from or similar to how a modern-day world leader might respond to news of war against his or her country?
2. Review the four-step strategy talked about in this chapter: 1. Seek the Lord; 2. Stand before the Lord; 3. Sing to the Lord; 4. See the salvation of the Lord. Did any part of this strategy stand out to you as being something you already do when you are fearful? If so, which part?
3. Seeking the Lord: It's interesting to note that even in a time of great distress, the first part of Jehoshaphat's prayer was not about his people's fear or a list of what they wanted. What was the focus of the first several sentences of his prayer? What affect do you think this might have had on his people?
4. Standing before the Lord: What do you think it means to wait on the Lord? Read Isaiah 40:31. If time allows, do a word study on the words *wait for* and *renew*. You should find these meanings:
   - wait for = (6960) qavah; to bind together
   - renew =(2498) chalaph; to change; substitute

   Thus, the verse could be translated as: "Those who are bound together with the Lord will exchange their strength for his." What encouragement does this bring to you?

5. Singing to the Lord: When do you have the easiest time singing God's praise? When is it the hardest for you? Do you ever find strength through praising God? How?

6. Seeing the salvation of the Lord: Talk about the condition the author described as being "spiritual agnosics." Do you identify with this idea? What strategies do you use to work at seeing what God is doing around you? Or does this just come naturally to you?

7. What did you think of the story of the son with Fragile X syndrome in the worship services? How would you respond to the mother's question: "When God sees us worshipping him, whom do you think he views as the retarded ones?"

8. Read through some of the verses referenced in Day Three of the study. Talk about any ones that had special meaning for members of the group. Ask if anyone has other verses they use to help them deal with fear.

Remember It

If your group is larger than six, break down into smaller groups (no more than five or six in one group). Then do the following:

1. Pair up so you can say your memory verses to one another. Explain why you chose that particular verse.

2. Share with your group a battle you are currently facing. How have you been reacting to this battle? Is there a different approach based on what you learned this week? What are some possible ways you can implement Jehoshaphat's strategy?

3. Discuss what you learned about God through this study. Then spend some time sharing prayer needs. Pray for one another to seek the Lord in the midst of our battles.

Amos: A blue-collar guy
The Book of Amos

Read This First

Through the study of Amos, relate Israel's wake-up call to our own situation.

Relate to It

Ask the following questions. Be prepared to participate.

1. List as many oxymorons as you can think of. Here are some ideas to get you started: *jumbo shrimp, clearly misunderstood, crash landing, civil war.*

2. Comfortable Christianity is an oxymoron as well, but it's one many Christians would like to follow. Look up the following verses and discuss the level of comfort found in each: Matthew 16:24; Luke 14:26; 2 Timothy 3:12.

3. What makes your Christian walk comfortable? What makes it uncomfortable?

Reflect on It

Amos was called out of his comfort zone in a number of ways, to speak an uncomfortable message. Discuss his story with the following questions.

1. Review what was going on in the northern kingdom of Israel. What had Jeroboam been doing? Refer to 1 Kings 12:25-33 as needed.

2. What kinds of things have Christians (or people who have claimed to follow Christ) been known to do in order to make worship more comfortable for people? Do you find any of these actions questionable? Explain your answers.

3. Discuss the sins that Amos spoke against. He talked about unjust actions against the needy and the oppressed. What kind of injustice towards these groups is happening in our country today? Do you think Christians could do more to fight against this? What?

4. We don't have to go far to find examples of immorality in our own society. First Peter 1:15 calls us to "Be holy because I am holy." What do you think this means for you? What responsibility do Christians have to limit immorality in their own lives? In their churches? In their communities?

5. LeAnne says if we looked at her checkbook and calendar, we could tell where her priorities lie, both good and bad. What about you? What would your checkbook and calendar tell us?

6. Do you agree with LeAnne's statement that "living *in* luxury is one thing, but living *for*

luxury is another"? Have you ever experienced luxury? What about it did you find alluring? Is there any downside to living in luxury?

7. Have you ever been called a hypocrite? Have you ever called someone a hypocrite? What is it people often find hypocritical about Christ followers today?

8. If you look back on your life, or perhaps on the lives of loved ones, can you recognize any patterns of behavior that keep being repeated? If those patterns have led to dark places in a loved one's life, have you been willing to confront that person about this? Why or why not? Do you see patterns in your own life of ways God has continued to reach out to you?

9. Are you able to see and feel God's love through his justice? What does this look like in your life?

Remember It

If your group is larger than six, break down into smaller groups (no more than five or six in one group). Then do the following:

1. Pair up so you can say your memory verses to one another. Explain why you chose that particular verse.

2. Share with your group one way in which you feel inadequate to do what God is asking you to do. Discuss what you learned about God through this study. Then spend some time praying for the areas where each person feels lacking, that they would have the faith to depend on God to supply what they need for whatever task he has for them to do.

Haggai and Zechariah: Prophets with a Purpose
Haggai 1, 2; Zechariah 4

Read This First

Understand the messages given to Israel by Haggai and Zechariah and relate their relevance to our lives today.

Relate to It

Ask the following questions. Be prepared to share a story from your own experiences.

1. What projects do you currently have unfinished?
2. What prevents you from completing them?

Reflect on It

Haggai and Zechariah were prophets used by God to remind the Israelites of their purpose. Discuss the following questions in connection with the messages they communicated.

1. Review the historical context. Why had the rebuilding of the temple stopped? (Read Haggai 1:3, 4; Ezra 5:1, 2; 6:14.)

2. Review the four messages of the prophets. First, consider your ways: What distractions keep you from spiritual growth? What things prevent you from serving God first?

3. Consider your God: What characteristics of God are presented by Haggai? (See 2:1-9.) Which of these have the most impact on the way you think about God?

4. The message of God to the Israelites was that he was with them and in them, and his glory was more than enough to fill the temple they were building. LeAnne writes that "God shifted their focus from the temple's shell to the one who filled it with his glory." How often is your focus more on the outside of your temple, your body, than on the inside? How often is it more on yourself than the one who fills you up? What can you do to switch your focus around when you need to?

5. Consider your efforts: The people of Israel were unclean, and so the work of their hands was not blessed (Haggai 2:10-19). All they needed to do was to return to God. Why is that so hard sometimes?

6. Think of some other Bible characters who had lost their focus and had to be brought back to task. How did God get their attention? (e.g., Jonah, David, Pharaoh, etc.)

7. Look at the role models from Scripture presented in Day Three. What do you notice

about them? What do they have in common? What is different?

8. Finally, consider your task: Read Zechariah 4:6-10. Have someone summarize in her own words what encouragement the Lord gave to Zerubbabel. How would you offer this message of encouragement to someone else who is struggling with priorities and focus?

Remember It

If your group is larger than six, break down into smaller groups (no more than five or six in one group). Then do the following:

1. Pair up so you can say your memory verses to one another. Explain why you chose that particular verse.

2. Which of the four "consider" messages spoke loudest to you this week? Why? Share as time allows.

3. Spend time sharing prayer needs. Pray for one another to keep our focus on God and the tasks he has called us to do.

Wife, mother, volunteer, career woman, teacher, speaker, leader, follower, author, military spouse, and friend—these are just a few of the roles LeAnne Blackmore has filled. She has cherished each of these and is encouraged to know that God's plan and purpose includes ordinary people like her being used by an extraordinary God like him!!

Born and raised in Michigan, this Yankee became a southern girl when she attended Milligan College in Tennessee. After graduation, she married her husband Ron and together they have two children, Spencer and Averie. LeAnne currently serves as Advisor for the Women's Ministry team at First Christian Church in Johnson City, Tennessee, and leads a weekly Precept Bible study.

A passionate speaker, LeAnne travels to women's retreats and conferences to communicate her desire to see women deepen their love for God and his Word. To find out more about LeAnne and her ministry, go to www.leanneblackmore.com.